What law enforcement professionals are saying about
***Emotional Survival for Law Enforcement* . . .**

"I have been through Dr. Gilmartin's ***Emotional Survival*** training at least twice in my career and I found his lessons on surviving a law enforcement career the most valuable tool to my success and emotional survival both professionally and personally. . . . This book should be required reading for all new police officers and their loved ones."

Douglas L. Bartosh
Chief of Police and Director of Public Safety
Scottsdale, Arizona

"The unique and increased value of this book . . . is that it can easily be revisited periodically. There are many occasions where reading (and rereading) this book can be immensely beneficial—these include when an officer is hired, reassigned, and/or promoted. From a command perspective, this book provides insights which can directly influence how certain management decisions are made and, sometimes more importantly, delivered. Finally, this book provides guidance to agency heads and senior management as to the tone that must be set in order to increase survivors and decrease victims within their organizations."

Ann Marie Doherty
Superintendent
Boston Police

"As a twenty-six-year veteran of law enforcement, I have had the opportunity to read many books and observe many trainers. ***Emotional Survival*** is a work of art! This book is perhaps the best law enforcement–related reading I have ever experienced. Whether you have twenty minutes on the job or twenty years, this book will make you a better officer and a better person, and just might save your life. Any person who wears a badge must read this book to better understand the climate of the profession. Dr. Kevin Gilmartin's experience and background in this field make him a definite asset to the law enforcement community and their families. Kevin has hit a home run with ***Emotional Survival,*** and will ultimately impact thousands of lives."

Sergeant Alan Green
Los Angeles Police Department
Past President, National DARE Officers Association

"If you are a law enforcement officer concerned you are losing the spirit and passion that attracted you to this career, or a leader concerned about the attitude and well-being of your troops, then you will profit from the common sense lessons of this book.

Dr. Kevin Gilmartin is nationally recognized not only for his groundbreaking work on the emotional survival of law enforcement officers, but also for his unique ability to captivate and personalize his message to a room full of cops. From his classroom comes this book, which captures the essence of the concepts and includes true stories which bring life to Gilmartin's material.

To this day, I remember glancing toward some of my grizzled sergeants as Gilmartin spoke. From the expressions on their faces, I knew Gilmartin's words were reaching them on a personal level.

Later, several of these supervisors openly acknowledged that Gilmartin was describing them and their life. The timing could not have been better, as our department was six months into a complete organizational change. To say officers and their supervisors were not happy with the reorganization is an understatement. Indeed, many supervisors saw themselves as victims, reeling from a new role, wearing newly designed uniforms and responsible for meeting new expectations.

A twenty-year cop himself, Gilmartin speaks a language cops can relate to. Supervisors were unanimous in their recommendation to bring Gilmartin back to address all our officers, which we did with as much success.

My concern on Dr. Gilmartin's departure was sustaining what we had achieved. Months from now, I wondered, would we fall back into the same old behavior patterns and again see ourselves as victims? While the old behavior patterns did not return to previous levels, it was clear we needed a resource to periodically revisit the concepts of emotional survival.

Dr. Gilmartin's book, *Emotional Survival for Law Enforcement*, is the tool we need to keep focused on the emotional well-being of our personnel. In addition, it provides those uninitiated to Gilmartin's concepts the opportunity to experience his dynamic class as he guides us step-by-step through the personal challenges faced by every cop.

Armed with Gilmartin's book, officers can learn to successfully cope with one of the toughest jobs in a free society. Law enforcement can be a rewarding career that leaves one fulfilled, not bitter, caring, not isolated, and most important, a survivor, not a victim. Gilmartin's work is a significant tool to help us achieve this goal.

Mention 'survival class' to a young officer and he will invariably assume you are speaking of 'street survival.' Gilmartin makes a compelling case that an officer's emotional survival is every bit as important. If we fail to recognize this fact, it is very possible that the end result may be the loss of an officer, not to the streets, but to his own lack of emotional coping skills. The combination of officers educated in emotional survival coupled with strong leadership dedicated to making these issues a priority will produce stronger organizations and healthier officers. This is the essence of Dr. Gilmartin's landmark book."

Paul N. Conner, Chief of Police
Round Rock Police Department, Texas
Retired Deputy Chief, Las Vegas Metropolitan Police Department

"I wish that someone would have talked about **Emotional Survival** with me during my career! Dr. Kevin Gilmartin's book would have helped me survive the politics of being a career cop. I certainly would have been better prepared to understand and help others as I rose through the ranks. Dr. Gilmartin's book should be part of the academy training as well as part of each and every promotional process. In fact, the politicians should read this."

Assistant Chief David S. Butzer (Retired)
Portland Police Bureau
Portland, Oregon

"**Emotional Survival** is an incredible book about the journey through the maze of police work. If you're a front line officer, supervisor, or command officer, you will see yourself in this book. It is the first book I have read that describes what really happens to police officers in their careers, with incredible insight into the stress and difficulties of being a police officer. Dr. Kevin Gilmartin sets out proactive strategies for police officers and their families to survive the most dangerous profession."

Brian Adkin
President, Ontario Provincial Police Association
Ontario, Canada

"The material in this book changes lives. It does so by affixing responsibility for one's life exactly where it should be, on the individual, removing "victim" status. We have seen miraculous, immediate changes in individuals who finally see who the real thief of their lives is—themselves. By following Kevin's advice, people become whole again. We, personally, and the law enforcement community, in general, owe Kevin a tremendous debt of gratitude for keeping us on track."

Barb Harris
Illinois State Police
and
Chief John W. Harris
Springfield Police Department, Illinois

"**Emotional Survival** should be required reading for all candidates and their families."

Edward Davis
Superintendent
Lowell Police Department, Massachusetts

"Having listened to Kevin Gilmartin over the years, I fully embrace what he states. Because the other day, I watched a young officer die. His death came about slowly over several months, but I am sure that it started a long time ago. He did not die a physical death but a professional one.

Standing in the holding area of the Clark County Detention Center, I watched as the police vehicles came and went. Then I looked up and saw one of my own officers under my command being led into the jail in handcuffs. He looked at me and I looked at him. I was looking for the young cop that he once was. He looked very scared. As we led him into the jail in which he started his career in law enforcement and put him through the booking process, I wondered what compromises he made. During that month, my officer was one of several in our agency that had been arrested for felony crimes. The arrest of the officers was of course the top story in the local media. They should be held accountable for their actions by our justice system.

Reality is that if we had several officers killed by gunfire in the line of duty in one month, the entire agency would be mobilized. I am sure that new training on tactics and officer survival would be rolled out. We would make sure that every recruit learned the lessons of the tragedy. In short, nothing would stop us from teaching the lessons to save the officers' lives on the streets.

But these officers died a professional death this month. We in law enforcement should be mobilizing. Every aspect of the officers' careers should be examined and the lessons learned should be taught to avoid future casualties. The lessons learned and taught about *Emotional Survival* need to be taught in every class of new recruits and to every officer working. The need to do so is great. We as a profession need to consider emotional survival as a part of officer survival."

Gary Schofield
Captain, Training Bureau
Las Vegas Metropolitan Police Department

EMOTIONAL SURVIVAL FOR LAW ENFORCEMENT

EMOTIONAL
SURVIVAL FOR
LAW ENFORCEMENT

A Guide for Officers and Their Families

Kevin M. Gilmartin, Ph.D.

E-S Press

Editing: Melanie Mallon

Design and
Production: Randy Schultz
                  DesignPro Graphics

Printed in the United States of America.

9 10—07 06

First printing, April 2002

ISBN: 0-9717254-0-3

Published by
E-S Press
8340 N. Thornydale Rd. #110-314
Tucson, Arizona 85741-1162

Library of Congress Control Number: 2002091277

This book is dedicated to the law enforcement professionals who serve and protect each of us daily. I only hope that in some small way it helps officers and their families complete the difficult journey through a law enforcement career with their relationships, families, and positive professional attitudes intact, and that it helps keep good people good.

Contents

Acknowledgements

I would like to express my appreciation to the following mentors, colleagues, and family members without whose guidance and support this book would not be possible: Col. Harold E. Russell, Ph.D., who was willing to share his accumulated wisdom earned over more than half a century as both a military and police psychologist and who helped direct the formative years of my professional career; Alexis Artwohl, Ph.D., and Chief David Butzer for their collegial review and suggestions; Melanie Mallon for her editorial expertise; Randy Schultz of DesignPro Graphics for his creative design of this book; Jennifer M. Gilmartin-Garnand, M.D., and Colleen F. Gilmartin, J.D., for the dedication and commitment they show to their respective professions and the value they add to their parents' lives; and Anne M. Baustian-Gilmartin, W.B.W., for her continuing love, support, and assistance over the last four decades.

Foreword

If you're a cop, you're going to love this book. It could change your life. It might even *save* your life, your career, your home life.

If you're not a cop, you'll still love it because the ideas in this book could certainly apply to you too. Maybe you're in a relationship with a cop or have a highly demanding career that puts you on the "biological rollercoaster" ride, a concept that stems from Dr. Gilmartin's brilliant insight into the cost of public safety work and other high stress occupations.

Author Kevin Gilmartin, Ph.D., is eminently qualified to write about emotional survival for law enforcement because he has lived it, studied it, researched it, and taught it. He is one of America's very few "cop docs." After earning his Ph.D. in clinical psychology, he was a career deputy sheriff with the Pima County Sheriff's Office (PCSO), in Arizona. He began work at Pima County in 1974, retiring from the sheriff's department in 1995.

In 1982 he was nationally recognized for his work in hostage negotiations when he was selected as one of America's ten best "Police Officers of the Year" by *Parade Magazine*. Other operational activities during his deputy sheriff career included assisting investigators, criminal profiling, crisis interventions with emotionally disturbed persons, and dealing with extremist groups. The article he wrote on religious extremist groups, "The Lethal Triad," is still used in counter-terrorism training.

A true police psychologist is a rare breed in itself, and Dr. Gilmartin was one of the early pioneers in this highly specialized area. He was invited to write articles for leading publications and developed one of the nation's earliest police behavioral sciences units in the Tucson metro area. Although his initial interest was in operational work, his work in counseling police officers and their families soon led him to the realization that one of the most critical and ignored areas in law enforcement is the emotional toll this stressful occupation takes on its own people, and his focus turned increasingly to this area.

As a deputy sheriff and doctor living, working, and studying the unique world of cops and their families, he developed a penetrating insight into the daily work life of cops. He came to see how it insidiously dismantled the personal lives, health, happiness, and careers of officers who weren't prepared to cope with the unique demands of the law enforcement lifestyle. These officers and their family members became emotional casualties. Dr. Gilmartin was determined to do something that could help them become emotional survivors instead.

Fortunately for law enforcement at large, Dr. Gilmartin is a gifted trainer who started training early in his career and soon became inundated with requests for training from all across North America. After retiring from the PCSO, he was able to devote all his efforts to taking his message on the road internationally and is teaching as many officers as he can about the hazards of the wild biological rollercoaster ride, a ride that can end in disaster if officers don't learn to manage it.

I first heard Dr. Gilmartin speak at the International Association of Chiefs of Police (IACP) conference in 1993. I was instantly impressed by two things: This guy really *knows* what he's talking about, and he is *fun* to listen to. Not only is he highly entertaining, his message is clear, straightforward, and easy to understand. His life-changing advice is practical and simple to apply once you understand the concept of the Hypervigilance Biological Rollercoaster®.

When he isn't helping cops, Dr. Gilmartin chases steers and enjoys the cowboy lifestyle on his small horse ranch in Arizona. He and his wife, Anne, are avid team ropers.

As a law enforcement trainer myself, I, like Dr. Gilmartin, travel all over North America training cops. Because I admire his work, I usually mention Dr. Gilmartin's name and encourage officers to attend his training if they get the chance. Time after time officers have come up to me during the breaks to tell me they had been fortunate enough to listen to Dr. Gilmartin speak in person or on his videotape. They rave about how entertaining and informative the class was, but, more important, they tell me that hearing him speak changed their lives. Many of the older veterans wistfully tell me, "Better late than never, but I wish I had heard his talk at the beginning of my career."

Now Dr. Gilmartin has put his message in print in a book that is not only profound but almost as entertaining as he is in person. So enjoy, and go become an emotional survivor.

—Alexis Artwohl, Ph.D.
Coauthor of *Deadly Force Encounters*

The Journey through Law Enforcement

F or many men and women, the actual journey through a law enforcement career begins with the arrival of the letter announcing acceptance into the upcoming recruit academy class. With the exception of the actual day of academy graduation, this letter may bring on one of the happiest moments of a law enforcement officer's career. Receiving word of acceptance into the academy signifies both a major accomplishment and a starting point. After months, maybe years, of trying—studying, testing, taking oral boards—recruits finally have a chance to start their careers as officers, careers they may have wanted for some time and ones to which they will demonstrate significant commitment and dedication. Enthusiasm, idealism, and motivation are the emotions of the day.

These positive emotions remain throughout the demands of academy training, and they carry the recruits through a physically and mentally challenging few months. Endless hours of classroom instruction, academic tests, and training in physical fitness, defensive tactics, pursuit driving, and firearms all combine to fill the next few months of the police recruit's life. Although the academy experience is demanding, both physically and mentally, police officers in training see it in a positive light. This starting point is full of new experiences and new relationships. Recruits eagerly await graduation day and the chance to get on the streets. Graduation day itself is a time of high spirits, during which recruits feel both a tangible sense of accomplishment for getting through the academy and the promise that an exciting and fulfilling career is just beginning.

The relationships among new recruits, formed during the trying times at the academy, can flourish over years of shared service as officers on the streets—often they develop into lifetime friendships. The intensity and extent of the relationships that occur among officers can be found in few other occupational fields. In spite of the positive and supportive nature of the friendships that typify the early stages of a police career, however, not all changes taking place in the new officer's world are equally positive.

One of the first costs of the journey through a police career can be the old friendships, the ones that predate police work.

One of the first costs of the journey through a police career can be the old friendships, the ones that predate police work. These friendships can be put on the back burner, and over time, these nonpolice friends may perceive their old friend, now an officer, as pulling back, not available, or only running around with cop friends. Sometimes these friendships are the first loss brought on by police work, but this loss typically goes unnoticed by the new officer, who is caught up in an exciting new career.

Learning on the Job

Law enforcement is an entirely new world for the young officer. Not only is the career new, the job itself is fun with a capital *F*. New officers focus on their mission to be the best officers they can be. They have so much to learn to become competent officers, most of which they learn from the older cops, the ones who have been there and done that. The older officers have paid their dues and are in a position to assist the young officer in obtaining full citizen membership in the police culture.

The reality is that although these more experienced officers really do know how to work the streets, often, tragically, that's the only part of their lives that does work effectively. When older officers are on the job, they know how to make decisions and handle situations. They appear competent and confident. Because the rookies' focus is almost exclusively on learning the job, they may see the shortcomings and failures in the veteran officers' personal lives as insignificant, if they notice them at all. From their predecessors, the next generation of officers learns how to handle the streets, but not necessarily how to handle their *lives* as officers. These veteran cops point the way and guide the journey from rookie to experienced fellow officer; however, the message passed along by veterans, many times, is an incomplete message for the overall transition. It focuses primarily on how to do the job—how to become a fellow cop who can be trusted and counted upon under extremely demanding situations. The trust of other cops does not come easily for the rookie officer—earning it can be an uphill battle. For some new officers, the transition to the streets is significantly harder than the previous demands of the academy. Being accepted and trusted by the other officers is, for most new officers, the major goal during the first year or two of their careers. This goal is earned only when the younger officers can demonstrate that they can be counted on in tough situations, that they can be trusted when the chips are down.

Idealistic Rookie to Cynical Veteran

As the new officer's career continues, he or she can learn to rely, almost exclusively, on the support and friendship of other officers, a tendency that begins during the intense bonding at the academy. The officer doesn't make a conscious decision to abandon old friendships—it's just a matter of time before they seem to fade away. There are so many things to do and learn and so little time left for socializing with old friends. As the first year of the career draws to a close, officers may find themselves distant and alienated from social networks and friendships that existed prior to joining the force. As the years of a police career continue to pass, officers can experience social isolation from *everyone* except other cops. Positive outlooks and emotions are often replaced by dark, moody, negative views of the world. Although officers can experience their professional lives growing and expanding, on too many occasions their personal lives become fragmented and disrupted. Although work relationships can be supportive and available, personal relationships can become strained, distant, and dysfunctional. For almost all law enforcement officers, the career begins from a position of enthusiasm, motivation, and idealism, but the journey over the years from new recruit to experienced officer produces changes. Idealism can become cynicism, optimistic enthusiasm can become pessimism, and the easygoing young recruit can become the angry and negative veteran police officer.

The Job, the Whole Job, and Nothing but the Job

Anyone exposed to the police experience, either as an officer or someone who cares about an officer, can comment on how this journey through the law enforcement career produces changes in the person. The job takes on more and more of the officer's time and becomes more than just a job—it can become the central and defining aspect of the officer's life. Without insight into what changes are taking place, the significant people in the officer's personal life can find themselves pushed aside, searching for a way to adapt to these changes or risk losing the relationship. Marriages are strained—some break. Children are all too often alienated from parental emotional support. The spouse or parent dimension of the new officer's life can become secondary to the cop dimension. The new officer can become emotionally distant, hardened, or physically absent from the lives of the people sharing the journey through the police career from the home front.

> *The job takes on more and more of the officer's time and becomes more than just a job—it can become the central and defining aspect of the officer's life.*

These changes taking place in the new officer's life are often alluded to or spoken of in the police culture, but rarely, if ever, are these changes seen as a major priority to correct. Very rarely are the changes in a new officer's personal life seen as anything but inevitable. Recruits are told that the job takes its toll, but they are hardly ever told or shown how to minimize the negative effects of the journey through the police career. Helping officers keep their personal lives intact is not a priority for many law enforcement agencies. Typically, agencies give no strategies or preventive game plans to the recruit.

These changes are not a problem isolated to a few law enforcement officers. These changes impact many new officers and families. Evidence of these changes are apparent by looking around any law enforcement agency and seeing the wreckage, both personal and professional, affecting the lives of many officers and police families.

Emotional Changes Lead to Physical Changes

The changes in officers' lives are not limited to their emotions or worldview. The emotional changes take place first: Anger can become a prevailing and ever present state in a police home. Then, as the years pass, physical changes can begin to appear. The constant anger and the physical upheaval it causes, combined with years of shift-work-induced sleep deprivation, poor diet, and a sedentary personal lifestyle, can lead the now veteran officer to face physical changes in addition to emotional issues. Physical fitness and positive recreation can deteriorate and disappear from officers' lives. The veteran officer can look back on the journey through the police career from a very different perspective compared to the one she or he held as a new recruit years before. The veteran officer can form two conclusions. The first may be a retrospective assessment of the journey:

> *"If I had to do it all over again, I don't think I'd become a cop. I'd go into some other line of work."*

The second conclusion of the veteran officer can take the form of a forward-looking formulation of long-off retirement plans:

> *"Ten more years and I'm the hell out of here."*

The officer's journey, all too often, takes its toll—a toll in worldview and outlook from positive to negative, from idealistic to cynical, from physically active and fit to sedentary and potentially unhealthy.

The cost of the journey can be measured in many ways. Professionally, minor dissatisfaction with the organization or agency can become all-consuming anger, hostility, and open hatred toward the management hierarchy of the police agency. The cost, unfortunately, can also be tabulated personally in failed marriages, children in trouble, and life views dominated by negativity, social isolation, and alienation from fellow human beings.

The veteran officer retiring after twenty or more years of service may not even vaguely resemble the positive, committed, and highly motivated recruit who began the journey. The scars, both physically and emotionally, are all too often clearly visible. Considering the potential costs of a police career to the officers themselves, their families, and the public they serve, what can be done to change this journey? What causes the changes, and can something be done to prevent or reduce the negative impact and damage to the officers and their families?

Officer Survival

2

Taking into account the old adage "If it's predictable, it's preventable," why are the predictable emotional changes and difficulties in an officer's life not prevented? Why aren't law enforcement organizations at least attempting major efforts to prevent the destructive effects on employees brought on by years spent as officers? Although many agencies do have dedicated police psychologists and employee assistance programs available, these traditionally have been focused on resolving issues once they develop, not on preventing them.

The law enforcement culture does, in fact, clearly value certain types of prevention and survival training. Any training that reduces and prevents physical injury and death to officers is highly valued. The focus of this training and preventive awareness, however, is on physical assault and injury. Keeping cops alive on the street is clearly the goal, which is understandable. After all, those injuries are visible, tangible, and immediate. Every police officer and those who care about police officers would agree that the development of professional skills in the area of officer safety is the most basic necessity. No one would argue against the need for significant investment of training resources in the area of officer safety to maximize street survival skills. Attendance at any police memorial service shows how lethal police work can be and the price that agencies, communities, and, most important, families pay in terms of officers' lives. Unfortunately, the development of skills to survive the emotional

> *Street survival and officer safety training must be the number one training priority; however, officer safety does not have to be the* **only** *training priority.*

aspects of a police career is given far less, if any, attention relative to the development of skills to survive the physical assaults of police work. Street survival and officer safety training must be the number one training priority; however, officer safety does not have to be the *only* training priority.

Survival Training Works

The development of officer safety training as a legitimate area of expertise over the past two decades has produced significant results and has saved many police officers' lives. This excellent survival training has resulted in significant reductions in the number of felonious line-of-duty deaths experienced by police officers over the last few decades. Although the number of officers policing the United States has grown significantly over the past four decades, the number of those officers dying feloniously continues to reduce (see the box below). This is the result of good cops practicing effective officer safety.

Law Enforcement Felony Deaths

• 1970	100	• 1986	66
• 1971	129	• 1987	74
• 1972	116	• 1988	78
• 1973	134	• 1989	66
• 1974	132	• 1990	66
• 1975	129	• 1991	71
• 1976	111	• 1992	64
• 1977	93	• 1993	70
• 1978	93	• 1994	79
• 1979	106	• 1995	74
• 1980	104	• 1996	61
• 1981	91	• 1997	70
• 1982	92	• 1998	61
• 1983	80	• 1999	42
• 1984	72		
• 1985	78		

Source: "Homicide Trends in the United States," Bureau of Justice Statistics, www.ojp.usdoj.gov/bjs/homicide/leok.htm

---

In spite of being faced with increasing gang activity, readily available automatic weapons, and a court system imparting questionable consequences for criminal activity, police officers are surviving the streets. Making officer safety training a high priority, combined with advancements in technology and equipment, such as improved ballistic vests and communications systems, have produced an increased chance of survival for officers confronting lethal threat. This form of training is accepted and valued in the police culture. Officers take a personal sense of ownership and responsibility for the development of their officer safety skills while working in the street environment. The number one priority for street officers is "stay alive so you can go home after shift." The culture takes officer safety so seriously that cops will refuse to work with an officer who repeatedly practices poor officer safety. It is culturally the highest priority.

Are Officers Really Surviving?

Officer safety training, no matter how essential and valid, does not have to be the only training priority. It does not need to be at the expense of training in the realities of the emotional effects of the career. Street survival training itself does not address the full picture of risk exposure for police officers. Although in many ways officers are winning the battle of street survival, they appear to be fatally losing the battle of emotional survival. An average of sixty-nine law enforcement officers died feloniously in the United States each year during the 1990s, but according to the National P.O.L.I.C.E. Suicide Foundation, police suicides averaged more than 300 per year during that same decade—more than *four times* the felony death rate (G. Fields, "Suicide on the Force," *USA Today*, June 1, 1999, p. 1A). This numerical difference between felony death and suicide should raise significant concern among both police officers and agencies, but unfortunately this startling information often falls on deaf ears.

Although in many ways officers are winning the battle of street survival, they appear to be fatally losing the battle of emotional survival.

The loss of even one police officer's life to a felony is unacceptable in the police culture. Police officers and agencies do everything within their combined power to increase officer survival. Training, equipment, and resources are dedicated to reducing felony death. Yet the suicide rate for police officers is three times the national average (T. Baker and J. Baker, "Preventing Police Suicide," *FBI Law Enforcement Bulletin*, October 1996, pp. 24–27). Over the same decades that law enforcement officers have been making strides in street survival, from 1950 to 1990, the suicide rate among police officers has doubled (J. M. Violanti, "The Mystery Within: Understanding Police Suicide," *FBI Law Enforcement Bulletin,* February 1995, pp. 19–23).

There does not appear to be a systematic recognition by agencies or officers of the emotional toll of police work and its contributing effect on self-destructive behavior.

The reports that indicate police officers have a significantly higher suicide rate than the general population are even more alarming when you consider that it is general practice in most police agencies to conduct pre-employment psychological evaluations of potential officers to rule out the pre-existence of psychological abnormalities before hiring. With the major efforts police agencies put into pre-employment screening of police applicants, it should be reasonably safe to assume that officers begin their careers psychologically more stable, physically more fit, and with fewer ongoing significant emotional crises than the general population. Why does the law enforcement profession face such alarming reported rates of self-destruction?

But That Can't Happen to Us

Some officers will look at the reported rates of suicide among law enforcement and rationalize:

> *"That's big city cops. I work in a small town and that kind of stuff doesn't happen here."*

That is denial hard at work attempting to make it easier on officers and agencies not to put the emotional survival of all personnel on the front burner. The Fraternal Order of Police (FOP) represents law enforcement professionals from agencies of all sizes. Of the 600,000 police officers on active service in the United States, the FOP represents 270,000. It is the nation's largest police association and it should be commended for its courage to take a hard look at the issue of suicide within its membership ranks. Compared to the average U.S. suicide rate of 12 per 100,000 (as reported by the Centers for Disease Control and

Prevention), the FOP found rates among officers that were alarmingly high: 22 per 100,000 officer members.

Fraternal Order of Police Death Rates
Between 1992 and 1994, 38,000 FOP members submitted life insurance claims for unnatural death:

37% Suicide

26% Homicide

6% Motor Vehicle Accidents

11% Other Accidents

Suicide isn't the only form of self-destruction: Depression, social isolation, and chronic anger also lead to the destruction of many other aspects of officers' lives that are not so readily visible. The journey through the police career clearly takes its toll. Suicides are just the extreme tip of the iceberg of emotional damage. Unfortunately, even this most extreme measure of psychological despair can be denied and rationalized away by the average officer and agency:

"Too bad about Joe. He just let this job get to him."

"Not everybody is cut out to be a cop."

"You got to know when to get out of here before you start thinking of eating your gun."

"Don't ever let this job get you that messed up."

"I thought Pat had her head screwed on tighter than that."

"What was wrong with him to do something like that to his kids?"

These statements can be heard at police agencies after a friend or fellow officer has taken her or his life. The surviving coworkers' statements are designed to make sense out of what happened and to put a safe distance between themselves and the officer who has committed suicide. Suicide by a healthy fellow cop can represent an act that the officers many times do not understand.

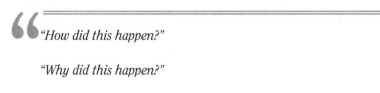

"How did this happen?"

"Why did this happen?"

"Did we miss something?"

Officers will ask these questions again and again in the time immediately after a police suicide. As the immediate sense of loss and bereavement lessens for the cops, however, the questioning diminishes. Any personal or organizational changes to be made and possibly any lessons to be learned from the tragedy are usually lost as everyone returns to the fast-paced world of police calls to answer and services to provide.

Denial Can Be Deadly

After a fellow cop commits suicide, many officers have to develop strategies to avoid acknowledging the real emotional impact the job can have. Officers design techniques to blunt and deny the realities. This means putting emotional distance between what happened and the world the officer still works and resides in everyday. In order to keep the suicide of a fellow officer at a safe emotional distance, fellow officers must tell themselves that the suicide must have been the result of some flaw in the individual psychological makeup of the dead officer:

*"Something must have been going on in her life
that none of us knew about."*

"I thought Joe had it more together than that."

Keeping psychological distance between the events that lead to a fellow cop committing suicide and the events that affect the surviving cops is essential if the officers have to keep doing the job without any insight or strategy for emotional survival. Denial creates the belief that psychological distance exists between what was going on in the dead officer's life and what is going on in the lives of the remaining officers. This helps create an illusion that "I'm doing OK," and "that stuff doesn't apply to me." Basically, it is a primitive attempt to ignore the emotional changes caused by police work and to deny emotional vulnerability. It's an attempt to avoid acknowledging the darker side of police work, the down side of the job. Many times, the only acknowledged glimpse of the darker side of police work is this often-heard phrase:

> *"I started out my career loving it, but I am starting to hate it and count the time until I'm out of here."*

Both officers and agencies can rationalize suicide as an isolated tragedy reflective only of the events existing in the life of the deceased officer. But what about the loss and deterioration of other aspects of the police officers' emotional lives, such as the destruction of functional intimate relationships, the loss of productive and loving parental roles in their children's lives, or just the loss of being happy on a daily basis? The realities of these day-to-day losses are harder to keep distance from than a suicide and can be seen without exception in any police agency. These losses are much closer to home and much harder to deny. The suicide rate of police officers, although terribly tragic, is not nearly as numerically significant as the number of marriages that are lost and the number of children who grow up emotionally distant from their police parents and, unfortunately, who grow up experiencing the secondhand effects of a police career.

Cynicism, anger, isolation, and social distrust affect too many police homes. When a police family is discussing the neighbors, who possibly have a different opinion on an issue, the idea of differences of opinions is not discussed. It's easier just to conclude, "The neighbors are assholes." For the police officer and police family, the world becomes "full of assholes." For most police officers, the concepts of social isolation and cynicism aren't a problem; they are just "the way the world really is."

> "*If a 747 airliner with approximately 300 passengers on board crashed each year, the Federal Aviation Administration would ground 747s until the problem was discovered and corrected, yet we lose 300 police officers every year to suicide and we think that is just the cost of doing business.*"
> —Robert Douglas, National P.O.L.I.C.E. Suicide Foundation
> (quoted in G. Fields, "Suicide on the Force," *USA Today,* June 1, 1999, p. 1A)

The toll in suicides, lost families, and the lost emotional well-being of the men and women who set their career goals as public service, "to serve and protect," is absolutely unacceptable. Whose job is it to serve and protect the officers and their families from the emotional risks of the job?

Are the Changes Inevitable?

3

C an the journey through a law enforcement career be made easier, safer, and less emotionally damaging to the police officer? Is the young, idealistic police recruit forced to experience the deteriorating emotional changes brought on by the job? Is the recruit destined to undergo these changes without exception or hope of emotional survival? Does the new police officer have any hope of remaining an emotionally stable, physically fit individual who enjoys both a fulfilling career in police work and a functional and healthy personal life?

Many police officers, in fact, do survive emotionally and remain functional, healthy individuals after twenty or thirty years of police work.

Many police officers, in fact, do survive emotionally and remain functional, healthy individuals after twenty or thirty years of police work. Many police families remain loving, functional, and supportive. These families can be seen interacting with members of the general community—at community events, activities at their place of worship, and sporting events. If some officers are able to remain emotionally functional, every police family and law enforcement agency needs to ask some questions:

- How do these folks survive the job emotionally?
- Is it anything besides just lucky breaks?
- Can the agency help other officers to survive emotionally?
- Are police agencies making the emotional survival of their members an issue of highest priority?
- Are police unions and fraternal organizations addressing the issues of their membership's emotional well-being?

- Is emotional survival for law enforcement officers an ongoing point of professional discussion?
- How often are the police officers themselves permitted to review, through targeted training, the impact of the job on issues such as anger, racism, happiness, depression, and substance abuse?

The Role of Organizations in Emotional Survival

Although most agencies and unions have counseling services available for personnel *after* problems surface, typically neither police agencies nor unions make the emotional well-being of their officers a high priority from a prevention perspective. This can become evident when some high-profile event occurs in the community that throws the agency into a controversy. The events causing the controversy at a police agency, many times, relate to the behavior of some of its officers. A controversy surfaces pertaining to an allegation of officer misconduct: This could be an abusive-use-of-force complaint, a racial incident, an integrity issue, or possibly a tragedy revolving around domestic violence in a police family. The media picks up the controversy and reports the events, obviously using whatever spin best serves the needs of the media. Bad news sells papers. Now, however, in light of the controversy, questions do get asked of the police agency about what services are available for its law enforcement personnel:

- Are your officers psychologically screened before you give them guns?
- Do your officers have counseling available to them if they have a personal problem?
- Is there a substance abuse program available for the department members to use?
- Do your officers receive ongoing training in police ethics?

Defensive Reactions instead of Constructive Actions

The questions come from the media, the politicians, and the community. Sometimes the questions come fast and furiously. The media, after some highly publicized incident, can be seen at first as holding the police agency's feet to the fire in the area of the psychological well-being of its officers. Initially, the media questioning appears to be a genuine effort to produce change, a desire to obtain assistance for the officers and also to produce and demand change in the way officers conduct business, how the officers treat the public, how they treat minorities, or how they report or fail to report the evidence of wrongdoings by fellow police officers. At first brush, it appears these media and community inquiries might actually produce some benefit for the agency and the officers themselves. Maybe some changes actually will be implemented that will make the journey through a police career easier. Maybe better psychological and counseling services will be provided.

The media, however, typically reports from a fundamentally antipolice perspective. "Vilify the cops" is always a good strategy to sell papers. The inherent antipolice media perspective on most controversies revolving around police officers' behavior does not typically cause officers to step back and review how they are doing emotionally. Usually, the media reports do little more then cause the rank and file officers, as well as management, to circle the wagons and take a defensive perspective, reinforcing the idea in most officers' minds that

"The media really are a bunch of bleeding heart assholes."

"People in the community don't have any idea what working on the streets as a cop is really all about."

Missed Opportunities

Sometimes the crisis becomes a missed opportunity for labor and management to form a necessary partnership to enhance the help that could be available for officers and their families. On occasion, when a highly publicized incident occurs at a law enforcement agency, some elements of the organized rank and file of that agency can attempt to exploit the crisis or controversy to generate political fallout against the incumbent agency management, a payback for past labor-management disputes. Some more aggressive labor leaders consider the crisis situation a great opportunity to initiate a vote of "no confidence" against the chief. This is when the shouts can be heard:

"If it happened on the chief's watch, the chief should be held accountable."

It sounds good, but is this attitude really producing changes in how police officers will survive their careers emotionally? Does it really get more help or support for the officer's emotional well-being?

The agency's higher level management, when faced with a controversy concerning officer behavior or misconduct, will attempt to show the community that the "chief is addressing the issue"; however, just like the officers, the administration often takes a defensive position. The posture might look different, but the response is equally defensive, particularly if high-ranking department personnel are part of the controversy through either action or inaction.

"We are presently conducting an investigation of the alleged behavior of the officers in question, all of whom presently have been placed on administrative leave pending the outcome of the investigation."

Obviously, this position may clearly represent a necessary and genuine organizational attempt to increase accountability for its officers. However, even if genuine management action is taken concerning the controversial behavior of the officers, it usually represents a disciplinary reaction to the problem and fails to address correction *and* prevention. The agency deals with the symptoms but doesn't address the root causes of the problem. When controversies concerning officer behavior erupt, they typically indicate that an officer or group of officers have failed to survive the job emotionally. Unfortunately, both labor and management miss the opportunity to turn a negative experience into a positive outcome by assisting the officers. Inappropriate behavior erupts and both labor and management jointly fail to address the big picture. No one benefits from the emotional and behavioral devastation and crisis in the lives of police officers. The agency, the individual officers and their families, and the entire community experience a loss. On so many occasions, labor and management fail to form joint partnerships of mutual benefit to all the stakeholders involved and ask the questions that are in the mutual interest of all parties:

- Why did this happen?
- How do we make the journey through the career easier and more balanced emotionally for our officers?
- Was this entire crisis avoidable?
- Can some basic change in the emotional preparation and maintenance of law enforcement officers take place?
- Can we teach police officers to be emotional survivors, the types of officers who make it through a career remaining highly productive and effective as cops, yet having balanced and effective personal lives? Can the journey be made easier?

What Is Actually Taking Place?

B efore we can initiate assistance for law enforcement officers, we need to know exactly what changes an officer goes through. The best way to find out what changes affect police officers is to go straight to the source—ask the cops themselves:

- "Do you see the world differently now that you are an officer?"
- "Do you look at people differently?"
- "Do you read situations differently?"

Experienced police officers answer each of these questions with a resounding "Yes."

- "Yes, I see people differently."
- "You bet I look at things from a different perspective now that I am a cop."
- "Yes, I see things now I never saw before or even knew existed before I became a cop."

A Matter of Perspective

Most officers realize they see the world differently but have never stopped to assess just how differently they perceive things. They typically don't have time to worry about it. The people they spend the majority of their time with see the world pretty much the same way they do—these people, of course, are other cops. The need for officers to step back and take

> *The people they spend the majority of their time with see the world pretty much the same way they do—these people, of course, are other cops.*

a look at changes in their worldviews since becoming officers appears to be a total waste of time, absolute nonsense, little more than touchy-feely garbage. Real changes, however, have taken place.

Has Your Worldview Changed?

The following word-association exercise will help you become aware of changes in your outlook since becoming an officer. Don't worry: This test doesn't require anything psychologically abstract like looking at inkblots. It involves simply taking a look at the word that appears below and saying the first thing that comes to your mind.

scout leader

What was the first word that came to your mind? Did you say something like "pedophile," "child molester," or "sex offender"?

The vast majority of times officers take the above word-association test, their responses are negative evaluations of the term "scout leader." Most people, however, see this term in a positive light. When I try this word-association test on other groups of adults, such as service club members, I get a very different set of responses. Typically, the nonpolice groups respond to the term "scout leader" with something like the following answer:

> *"An adult man or woman interested in helping youth,*
> *primarily through outdoor activities."*

I have tested a large number of law enforcement groups and have never received that positive response from a group of officers. When I point out that their response is unique, some officers become defensive:

"Don't tell me it's some way that *I* see world. I don't know where you live, but let me tell you about the real world—it's the way the world is. Every scout leader I have ever met has been a pedophile. Normal adults don't hang out with kids."

Before condemning the officer as incorrect, it is important to review his response: "Every scout leader I have ever met has been a pedophile." He's probably exactly right. Every scout leader he has ever met has been a pedophile—odds are, so has every teacher he's ever met, every truck driver, or even every astronaut. He's a cop, in this case a sex-crimes detective—he doesn't meet normal people. He knows victims and he knows suspects. He is probably a subject matter expert in the law enforcement area of sex crimes. He knows a great deal about investigating sex crimes. He knows how to control a crime scene, preserve evidence, take statements, and prepare a case for presentation to the prosecutor to have the case issued and a warrant obtained. He knows his area of expertise. However, in terms of the whole world, how wide an area does the subject matter involved in sex crimes really cover? It represents a very narrow slice of the world. After a while, that narrow slice of the world, known as police work, can become the officer's entire worldview. The view is typically one of negativity, anger, violence, and trauma. Police officers have lots of data from which to draw conclusions about the world; however, as the years go by, because of the world the officers are immersed in, the data becomes more and more contaminated and so do the conclusions the officers draw.

Cynicism

Law enforcement personnel, like all other human beings, form their worldviews and predictions about life from the situations and events they see every day. Who calls the police to their home because things are going well?

Law enforcement personnel, like all other human beings, form their worldviews and predictions about life from the situations and events they see every day. Who calls the police to their home because things are going well?

Can you imagine a law enforcement dispatcher receiving the following telephone call for service from a citizen?

"Hello, police department? I just got home and I discovered the house is really clean and my spouse made a great meal for us and the kids all made the honor roll at school and we are even a little ahead financially. Please send some officers—and hurry!"

Even the thought of receiving such a call is ludicrous. People call law enforcement when things are not working out, not when things are going well. It has been said that officers see people at their baddest, maddest, and saddest. Is it any wonder that the officers' worldviews change?

Try the scout-leader test on even some subspecialty types of law enforcement officers, such as National Park Service rangers and Bureau of Land Management rangers. These are the men and women who provide law enforcement services on public lands. They are as much law enforcement officers as their city or county counterparts; the only difference is that the few thousand people a day who visit their "city" (the park or public recreation area) change each day. Ask rangers what comes to mind when they hear the term "scout leader" and the response many times is some offshoot of the following:

"An incompetent adult who marches youth to their deaths!"

What is taking place in the minds of these men and women that causes them to see things so differently from the average person? "Scout leader" for most people invokes an image of a caring and trustworthy adult. Why isn't this so in the minds of our law enforcement officers? Could it be the type of contact law enforcement officers have with a small number of scout leaders that shapes their entire worldview? Could the answer lie in the fact that police work makes people cynical?

Cynical: *Contemptuously distrustful of human nature and motive.*
—Webster's Collegiate Dictionary

Think for a moment of the world of the street police officer. Does being distrustful of human nature and motive have a purpose? Yes, it keeps cops alive. It is highly essential that every police officer—making every call for service, making every traffic stop—practice excellent officer safety skills, which translates into being distrustful. Officers don't know which traffic stop is going to culminate in an officer-involved shooting, so they have to be distrustful

Does being distrustful of human nature and motive have a purpose? Yes, it keeps cops alive.

of human nature and motive at each and every traffic stop and at *all* calls for service. This is common sense to the experienced police officer. What happens, however, when the distrust does not remain just an occupational observational skill-set that the officer has honed while working the street? What happens when the officer sees everything and everybody through the same filter of distrust? What happens when the officer's worldview is one of distrust? The officer arriving at this point is cynical. It's a mindset that works well on the street but wreaks havoc on one's personal life. No one is trusted, except, obviously, a few select cops.

"Everybody has an angle."

"Don't be naive. He's not as nice as you think he is."

This type of cynical outlook projects negativity into activities and social gatherings and can be extremely difficult on nonpolice friends and members of the officer's family. The officer can be viewed as negative, distrusting, hard, and unforgiving.

Ask police officers if they are cynical and most will respond:

"You bet I'm cynical. You would be too if you saw half the stuff I see everyday at work."

Ask officers' significant others if the officers have become cynical and you might get an answer similar to the following comment.

"My husband and I were on vacation recently with my parents. We were driving through a city about 100 miles from our home. My father was in the front seat with my husband, and my mother and I were in the back seat. My mother notices a teenage boy riding a new bicycle and she comments, 'Look, that boy has a nice bike,' to which my husband responds, 'Yeah, that means someone else doesn't have their nice bike anymore.' I ask my husband, ' Do you always have to be so negative?' and he says, ' Honey, I'm just telling it like it is.' "

—an officer's wife

When asked, officers admit to being cynical, but many times they are not aware of the long-term impact cynicism creates on attempting to maintain a normal social, family, and emotional life. There is a high cost to one's personal life by being cynical. The cost can be seen in how law enforcement officers view life in general.

The Cynicism Ratio

If you want to determine if you have become cynical, take this simple test of your individual cynicism ratio. The cynicism ratio will show numerically to what degree cynicism has invaded your worldview. To take the cynicism test, perform the following mathematical calculation:

Take the square root of the number of times you say "bullshit" on an average day.

$$\sqrt{\text{B. S.}}$$

Using the above equation, many officers would see both themselves and their fellow officers score highly on the cynicism scale each day. Any time something occurs that they disagree with, "it's bullshit." A memo arrives down the chain of command from the administration and before they even read it, officers respond with a chorus of

"Look at this bullshit. Don't they have anything better to do than micromanage the troops?"

As the years in a police career pass, anything and everything an officer disagrees with, doesn't like, or finds different is "bullshit." It comes in many varieties:

- political bullshit
- administrative bullshit
- affirmative action bullshit
- management bullshit (for union members only)

- union bullshit (for management only)
- touchy-feely bullshit
- total bullshit

The list could go on and on. It represents officers' anger, frustration, and growing intolerance of things that bombard them every day while doing their jobs as police officers. This can be observed daily at any law enforcement agency by listening to officers chant their daily mantra:

"Being a cop wouldn't be so bad if it weren't for all the bullshit."

The frustration and overwhelming need to turn it all off causes the officer to take a psychological shortcut by just labeling things "bullshit." It beats having to listen to people's problems every day at work— the same problems the officer has been listening to for the past five or ten years and probably will be listening to for the next ten or fifteen years. It's just easier to shut down psychologically and distance yourself from the events around you. Officers can put up protective shields and not be affected by the events around them. They don't have to think about things they disagree with. They just label them "bullshit" and move on.

Officers don't have to try to explain or deal with events outside their comfort zone. Creating this distance is a much less painful way of facing the emotional challenges of police work in the short run. Saying, "It's just bullshit anyway, don't worry about it," however, is not a very effective tactic in the long run for learning the skills to survive emotionally as a police officer. What happens to young enthusiastic and idealistic men and women when they begin thinking everything is bullshit? How long before the core values and idealism they brought to the job begin eroding and start seeming like meaningless, useless, and extremely naive ways of viewing the world that police officers see every day? And how long before this belief spreads to the remaining areas of an officer's life?

> *Officers don't have to try to explain or deal with events outside their comfort zone. Creating this distance is a much less painful way of facing the emotional challenges of police work in the short run.*

The Source of All the Bullshit

As cynicism develops, and everything becomes bullshit, the officer has to be able to explain the source:

Where does all this bullshit come from?
Who causes all this bullshit?

Soon an obvious answer appears. Every officer knows who causes all the bullshit:

The assholes.

Now the police officer, who is growing in both street experience and, simultaneously, cynicism, can explain any social dilemma or problem that presents itself:

"It's just bullshit and this guy is an asshole."

Now there is no longer any need to deal with the problems officers encounter every day. They just go through the motions because "it's just bullshit anyway." Anyone they don't agree with "is just an asshole." All "alternative life forms" are assholes. That means anyone officers don't like, don't trust, are uncomfortable with, or don't even know is an asshole. The longer someone is a law enforcement officer, the larger the number of assholes he or she knows. Fewer and fewer people in the officer's life are spared the label. By the time many officers are ready for retirement, they can count on one hand the number of people who are *not* assholes. Also, the more years someone is an officer, the more different varieties of assholes, or "proctological personalities," the officer discovers or creates. Because the term is reserved for anyone the officer doesn't trust, and many cops trust no one but a small inner circle of partners and friends, the world soon appears overpopulated with assholes. In order to keep the different varieties of assholes straight, officers many times creatively generate subtypes:

- known assholes
- flaming assholes
- management assholes (for union members only)
- union assholes (for management only)

- federal assholes (for local and state cops only)
- local assholes (for federal agents only)
- political assholes

The only thing limiting the creation of new categories is the imagination of the cops involved, but remember—cops can be very creative. What the term "asshole" really designates, for an officer, is an individual who causes the officer to experience a state of physical uneasiness or discomfort. This state of physical discomfort lets the officer know he or she is in potential jeopardy when this person, the asshole, is present. The jeopardy could be physical risk, occupational risk, or emotional risk. Early on in a police officer's career, the feeling of jeopardy is usually experienced only in street encounters, where physical risk occurs. The essence of street survival for police officers is the ability to appreciate the feeling of being in jeopardy in most situations and to use that feeling to enhance street survival skills. Feeling in jeopardy permits the officer to be prepared in case something potentially threatening occurs. This is the street survival mindset. As the years pass, however, the officer becomes quite competent in his or her street survival skills and the feeling of jeopardy comes mostly from people within the police agency, hence the often heard statement:

"I can handle the assholes on the street, I just can't handle the assholes running this agency."

It really means, "I feel more threatened by the people in management."

Taking Cynicism Home

Now, armed with these two concepts, the officer can be protected from the emotional battering experienced every day at work. They are very effective concepts if the officer's goal is to blunt feelings, avoid getting hurt, and function in a hostile world of negative experiences. But is the officer's entire world really full of negative experiences? What about at home?

How does this social alienation and cynicism affect the personal life of the officer? How does the officer who has not been given information or guidance on dealing with cynicism learn to live a balanced life? What happens when the officer's eight-year-old son wants to join the

Boy Scouts? How does the officer let the boy join an organization if she or he believes that all scout leaders are pedophiles? How does the cynical police officer function as a parent?

The following dialogue between parent and child demonstrates the impact of cynicism.

Child: *When we bought our pick-up truck, you said Fords are the best pick-up trucks.*

Parent: *That's right.*

Child: *Well, Johnny Jones down the street, his mom and dad just bought a new truck and they said Chevys are the best pick-up trucks.*

Now the parent has to take the time and energy to help shape the worldview of his or her child, to teach about differences of opinion and how to interact with people who think differently than the officer and his or her family think. Two basic response patterns are available in this straightforward parent-child interaction.

Parenting Response Option 1:
"Son, not everybody will agree with our opinions. Personally, we prefer Fords, but not everybody will prefer them. They have the right to believe differently than we do. We don't have to agree with them, but we have to respect their right to hold different opinions."

Parenting Response Option #2:
"Son, that's bullshit. Fords are much better trucks than Chevys. I think the Joneses are assholes and I don't want you going down there to play anymore."

Obviously, Parent Response Option 1 takes a lot more energy and willingness to engage the child in learning to appreciate and accept differences. How often would the cynical, tired, and angry police officer, without thinking, opt for Parent Response Option 2?

How often do officers let their anger and cynicism cloud their judgment, even in the way they speak to their children and families? Unfortunately, many law enforcement parents, without thinking, let their cynicism and social isolation dictate the very manner in which they admonish their own children:

"Quit acting like a little asshole!"

"If you don't straighten up, you're going to grow up to be an asshole!"

Not exactly Mr. Rogers' Neighborhood, but then again, most cops would probably think Mr. Rogers is an asshole.

Is Cynicism Unavoidable?

Is it a forgone conclusion that cops are cynical individuals who think most people are assholes? Is it unavoidable that police officers will believe the answer to most social dilemmas or questions is "who cares, it's just bullshit anyway"? Must this happen? Absolutely not! However, without effective training in emotional survival skills, both in the beginning of and throughout a law enforcement career, a cynical outlook is unfortunately the predictable result. Without taking time to make emotional survival a priority, many police officers' lives will be typified by a lifetime of cynicism-based thinking and decisions. The consequences of this type of thinking and interaction with children and loved ones are typically felt only years later in terms of failed love relationships and strained, or even broken, parent-child relationships that may never recover.

> *How often do officers let their anger and cynicism cloud their judgment, even in the way they speak to their children and families?*

Hypervigilance

5

What causes the psychological changes in law enforcement personnel? Is the negative, cynical, angry outlook that typifies many law enforcement officers directly related to and caused by the many tragic, negative, and violent events that an officer is forced to witness over the years of being a cop? Or is there something else occurring that affects the way law enforcement officers view the world?

Is it *what* cops see in the world?

Or

Is it *how* cops must learn to see the world?

Is there a unique perceptual set, or way of viewing the world, that officers learn? Do law enforcement officers need to see the world differently than most folks? Do they need to learn to see the world as potentially lethal in order to be safe as cops? Of course. Officers *must* learn to see the world differently than most folks in order to increase the odds of going home each day after work.

"If I see the world as potentially violent, I'll be prepared for violence if it does take place."

From the first day of academy training, through an entire career of police work, officers have to learn to perceive the world as potentially hazardous in order to survive the streets. Officers are exposed every day to a series of unknown events, any one of which could be perfectly harmless or lethally dangerous. Officers have to guess which event is safe and which event is lethal. An officer can make 10,000 traffic stops and 9,999 are perfectly safe; however, one can take his or her life—the officer just doesn't know which specific one is lethal and therefore must approach all 10,000 as potentially lethal. An officer making a traffic stop may be dealing with a family out for a drive or an individual with outstanding felony warrants. The officer has to figure out which is the case by reading unknowns.

Officers are exposed every day to a series of unknown events, any one of which could be perfectly harmless or lethally dangerous.

An old street adage states, "Bad guys don't wear name tags." Deciding which unknowns are harmless and which ones will prove to be lethal can be accomplished only by assuming that all the unknowns are *potentially* lethal unknowns until proven otherwise. An unknown situation can be proved harmless only after the fact. Officers reduce lethal threat by practicing this perceptual skill-set known as *officer safety*. All situations are potentially lethal until proved otherwise.

Central to the development of any officer safety skills is the understanding that officers not only must perceive the environment as potentially lethal, but also must accomplish this perceptual task immediately, when time is of the utmost essence. They must perceive the environment rapidly and accurately. Interpreting each unknown as potentially lethal permits the officer to have a greater sense of preparedness, regardless of how the unknown event actually plays out in the end.

Better Safe than Sorry

In any situation, an officer can misread unknowns and miss lethal warning cues. What starts out as something harmless or routine can cost officers their lives.

"Is that person reaching for his wallet or a weapon?"

Not accepting the potential risk in any situation is not practicing good officer safety. Not being perceptive of every nuance of the environment can prove lethal. It is better to approach a harmless situation prepared for risk than to approach the lethal situation unprepared. Experienced police officers know that it is important to err on the side of perceptual preparedness rather than perceptual laziness.

This is absolute common sense to experienced street officers. They learn it early in their career, and officers don't want to work the streets with someone who doesn't see the world from this cautious perspective. Officers will quickly comment on another officer's lack of street safety:

"They are just not safe to work with. Maybe they would be OK at a desk job, but not on the street. They are going to get someone hurt or killed."

This perceptual set of elevated alertness of the surroundings, which is required of law enforcement officers for survival, is referred to in the police culture as officer safety; however, a more accurate term would be *hypervigilance*.

Hypervigilance is the necessary manner of viewing the world from a threat-based perspective, having the mindset to see the events unfolding as potentially hazardous. The effective and safe street officer has to believe that every encounter possesses the potential of lethal risk. The perceptual set of hypervigilance lets the officer have an increased awareness of all the data available in the environment. As an officer makes a "routine" traffic stop, he or she needs to interpret the environment rapidly and accurately, asking the basic questions that reflect hypervigilance:

> *Hypervigilance is the necessary manner of viewing the world from a threat-based perspective, having the mindset to see the events unfolding as potentially hazardous.*

- Who is in the backseat?
- Where are everyone's hands?
- Where do I stand?
- Where do I move if this traffic stop goes bad and I have to defend myself?

Asking these questions is the necessary thought process of every effective law enforcement officer working in a street or risk environment. This perceptual set, which is required of effective police officers, has a biological dimension. The brain of the competent street police officer perceives the world from a perspective of hypervigilance. Rapid perception, quick interpretation of events, perceiving unknowns as potentially lethal until proven otherwise—these are all part of the hypervigilance mindset. The most important thing law enforcement officers do *every day* is go home to their loved ones after work *every day*. There is no such thing as too much officer safety.

Effects of Hypervigilance
How does this perceptual set of hypervigilance affect the officer psychologically over a significant course of time? In the short run, during the early years of a police career, it is a fun, exciting, stimulating mindset:

"Man, I love this job!"

This effect raises some questions:

- What about as the years go by?
- Does hypervigilance have effects on the officer's professional role?
- What are the effects of hypervigilance on the officer's personal life?

Can this perceptual set, that is so important for street survival, be the major contributing factor to the significant change emotionally affecting many police officers across the span of their law enforcement careers?

Hypervigilance permits the on-duty officer to develop the perceptual set required for maximum officer safety. Every decision the officer makes is dependent on the perceptual set of hypervigilance. Each of the officer's decisions on an event such as a traffic stop demonstrates the impact of hypervigilance on behavior. Each action the officer takes is controlled by the perceptual set of hypervigilance: positioning and movements, how close he or she permits the citizen to stand, requesting and then requiring the citizen on a traffic stop to step away from a vehicle or to step away from a potential weapon or item of threat. This perceptual set soon becomes the officer's way of perceiving the world. When describing effective law enforcement officers who practice hypervigilance, one could say:

"Good officers learn to see the world as one big felony in progress. They are just driving through it and they don't want any of it to splash on them."

This very necessary perceptual set of hypervigilance should be ever present in effective and safe law enforcement officers. It permits them to lower the potential risks to which they are exposed. Most people outside of police work do not need to develop a perceptual set of hypervigilance. The average citizen encounters an average level of daily risk. Most people have the luxury of "living between the lines," living within the normal range of emotion, risk, and reactivity to the environment. Living in the normal range of vigilance is a perfectly acceptable range for the average person dealing with a normal level of risk, threat, or demand. No need for most women and men to see the world as potentially threatening—if something goes wrong, they can just call the cops. The average person can quite comfortably approach life "between the lines," as shown in the figure below:

Normal Range of Risk

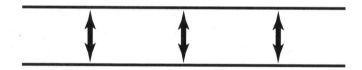

Average citizens can live in the normal range of risk—between the lines—usually without consequence. They can see the world as a basically safe and positive place. The average person does not need to experience hypervigilance on a daily basis. One might experience it on occasion—for example, walking down an unknown dark street in a bad neighborhood at night might permit the average citizen to experience hypervigilance. The unknown dark street presents many unknowns to the citizen. The average citizen might then begin asking the hypervigilance questions:

- Am I in harm's way?
- Is that person approaching me a potential assailant?
- Is that group of men following me?
- Is that a sound I hear behind me?

All of these questions are the evidence of the existence of a hypervigilant perceptual set.

"Let me pay attention to every sight, sound, and other sensory input available to increase my awareness of the environment and thus lower my chances of being victimized by an unknown."

The average citizen in the course of his or her daily routine rarely experiences hypervigilance. When a situation does develop that exposes citizens to some potential risk in their environment, they many times interpret the sensations as alertness, anxiety, or fear. The police officer experiences hypervigilance daily (or *should* experience it daily) if he or she is practicing good officer safety. It is the perceptual set that lets the officer see threat or risk before it takes its toll.

The Biology of Hypervigilance

What exactly is hypervigilance and how does it affect officers? Hypervigilance is a biological state. Its foundation is in the neurological functioning of the brain. The brain has a set of structures, known as the *reticular activating system (RAS)*, that determine the level of alertness that is necessary at any given time. Whenever the brain interprets the existence of a potential for threat or risk, the RAS engages the higher functioning levels of the brain into a higher level of awareness and perceptiveness of the environment. This response is meant to increase survival by enabling the brain to perceive potential threats before they take place. The increased level of alertness and awareness of the surrounding environment needed for officers to safely work the streets is caused by the hypervigilance response and produces an increased functioning of the sympathetic branch of the autonomic nervous system.

The *autonomic nervous system* controls the body's internal organs and automatic functions:

- pulse
- respiration
- body temperature
- blood pressure and other functions

The level and pattern of responsiveness of the autonomic nervous system is an individual's characteristic manner of emotional reactivity to risk, demand, or threat. It is the individual's basic physical level of reactivity to the environment, or the person's physical temperament. The autonomic nervous system is the biological aspect of the officer's sixth sense on the street—that capacity to be ready when something takes place or needs an immediate reaction, a reaction that just might keep the officer alive in a tough situation.

The autonomic nervous system is divided into two separate and opposite branches, the *sympathetic* and *parasympathetic* branches. The sympathetic branch is the part of the autonomic nervous system that reacts and controls bodily function in times of challenge or threat. This is the branch that is involved during the police officer's day-to-day functioning. It could be considered the "on-duty" branch. During hypervigilance, the sympathetic branch turns on those bodily functions that are required for physical survival. This biological state of hyper-vigilance is the body's way of increasing survival through heightened functions:

- increased peripheral vision
- improved hearing
- faster reaction times
- increased blood sugar
- elevated heart rate
- increased blood pressure
- a general sense of energy to meet and overcome any threats that are challenging the body's capacity to survive

When on duty, the hypervigilant officer operates above the normal range of risk, as shown in the figure below.

Hypervigilance

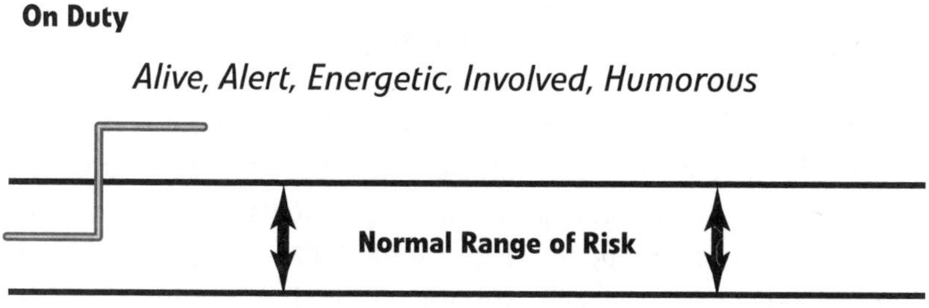

On Duty

Alive, Alert, Energetic, Involved, Humorous

Normal Range of Risk

Unlike the civilian, who can live between the lines, the on-duty officer is above the line. The officer is practicing good officer safety, is experiencing hypervigilance, and has a perceptual set of preparedness for engaging in the environment to survive potential threats. Inattentiveness to the environment is lethal for on-duty police officers. Early in a law enforcement career, as officers are being introduced to on-duty police work, they make a conscious decision about their need for hypervigilance and its increased alertness concerning their surroundings. New officers can express this decision using varying words, but it usually takes the form of a thought like the following:

"I better pay attention out here. I could get killed, I could get hurt, I could get somebody else hurt."

As mentioned above, the state of hypervigilance includes increased peripheral vision, more focused hearing, increased heart rate, and elevated blood pressure—all biological responses that enhance survival. The on-duty officer experiences this *objective* biological state as a subjective state of increased alertness, increased awareness of the environment, elevated sense of attention, more rapid thinking, and increased capacity to make quick decisions and think on one's feet. While in a state of hypervigilance, officers also display good senses of humor—good but usually rather sick. This state of alert interaction with the environment, at mild to moderate levels, is not unpleasant to experience physically. In fact, it feels rather good physically—at least for the first few years of a law enforcement career.

This state of alert interaction with the environment, at mild to moderate levels, is not unpleasant to experience physically.

"It's fun to be a cop."

This elevated level of nervous system arousal (arousal of the sympathetic branch of the autonomic nervous system) makes people feel alive, quick witted, and able to handle any problems. Law enforcement officers experiencing hypervigilance interpret it as a unique feeling that comes about when they begin working on the streets or in any potentially threatening environment. Because the effective street police officer needs to believe all encounters are potentially threatening in order to increase his or her chances of survival, it only follows that the officer will experience this elevated sense of perceptual arousal or hypervigilance in almost all police-related encounters. Officers feel alive, involved, engaged—they feel a sense of camaraderie with those men and women who share the risk involved in police work. One of the reasons police relationships are quite intense and the culture close-knit is that the men and women of law enforcement know the feeling of hypervigilance and it becomes the binding glue of the police culture.

> *Cops know what it feels like to be a cop. Just about everybody else is on the outside looking in.*

Cops know what it feels like to be a cop. Just about everybody else is on the outside looking in. The physical reactions and sensations of being a police officer are the defining parts of the culture.

How Others Perceive Hypervigilance

This aspect of the perceptual set of hypervigilance becomes inseparable from the police role. When an officer is engaged in a police-related activity, he or she experiences hypervigilance. People outside of police work observing hypervigilance many times cannot understand why the officers acted the way they did during any given encounter. The citizen unaware of the concept of hypervigilance and the survival behaviors it will produce in the law enforcement officer can draw a totally inaccurate conclusion when viewing the officer's behavior.

"The officer seemed so rude. He didn't walk up to my car so I could get a good look at him next to the driver's door. He stood back behind the driver's door, so I had to turn way around just to look at him and talk to him. He seemed very serious and unfriendly."

How often during encounters with the police do citizens view the officer as rude, judging by behavior such as standing slightly behind the driver's door during a traffic stop? From the officer's perspective, this is good officer safety. He or she is dealing with an unknown (the citizen) from a perspective of hypervigilance. The officer is watching every move the citizen makes to be able to react to any potential threat before it surfaces. Hypervigilance becomes the filter through which the law enforcement officer experiences the world. All situations are potentially lethal; all situations require attention, alertness, involvement, and quick intellectual assessment of the situation. All on-duty encounters require hypervigilance. The hypervigilant perceptual set is engaged not only while the officer is actually involved in an in-progress law enforcement encounter, it is engaged whenever the officer is observing the world. It is the *potential* of risk for which the officer must be prepared. Citizens often misunderstand hypervigilance and the behavior it generates among police officers:

"Why did it take four cops to talk to the driver?
He wasn't doing anything wrong."

This is a complaint from a citizen unaware of hypervigilance and how it necessarily drives officers' behavior. The citizen, many times, cannot appreciate that the officers did not know that the driver wasn't going to do anything wrong. For the officer, the entire situation and the people involved were unknowns. Hypervigilance saves cop lives.

The Appeal of the Hypervigilant State

From the beginning of their careers, each time officers put on the uniform and assume the police role, hypervigilance kicks in. A sense of alertness, aliveness, and quick decision making becomes the biological and psychological world of the on-duty police officer. Cops think well on their feet—hypervigilance sees to that. Cops know the feeling of being a cop. For many young officers, the feeling has a recreational sense about it. Many veteran officers who leave police work, for whatever reason, return to the job with the following explanation for their return to the field:

"Cop work gets in your blood."

This subjective state of hyperalertness and elevated thought and emotional responses becomes inseparable from the police role. Very few careers create hypervigilance in the work force. Very few careers have workers who begin their careers with such enthusiasm.

Very few careers create hypervigilance in the work force. Very few careers have workers who begin their careers with such enthusiasm.

"I love this job. I love being a cop."

New officers say that for the first few years, anyway. Watch young police officers at work and you will see people experiencing hypervigilance. New officers are often experiencing this reaction for the first time in their lives. They just can't get enough of doing the job.

Many people try to experience the hypervigilance of police work vicariously. What other career field has positions, such as many law enforcement agencies have, similar to volunteer or reserve officers? These are men and women who volunteer to attend the police academy, without pay, on their own time. They often incur many expenses for the tools of the trade, such as uniforms, weapons, and leather, out of their own pockets.

What do the reserve officers get for their contribution of time, energy, and commitment? Ask the reserve officer and you might get the more socially acceptable answer of "helping my community" or "trying to make a difference through public service." Get to know the reserve officer a little more personally and you get the real answer. She or he might not use the correct term, but the concept of hypervigilance is in the response:

"I get that alive, high-energy, quick-thinking feeling that makes the reds redder and the blues bluer."

What other career field offers chances for citizens to come out and share the workers' time without being compensated? What other career field has anything like citizen ride-alongs? What do the citizens get for their eight hours in a patrol car with an officer?

"I get a front row seat to the greatest show on earth."

Even on days that are uneventful, when the officer tells the citizen, "Sorry, tonight was kind of slow and you didn't get to see very much," the citizen is thinking, "Are you kidding? I got to see all kinds of stuff." What other career field offers this sense of aliveness, engagement, and quick thinking at work? What other career field engages that constant state of elevated alertness, even when nothing is taking place, because the potential for risk always exists?

On the flip side, what other career field also offers the depression, exhaustion, and desire for social isolation that can typify a law enforcement officer's life at the end of each workday? Hypervigilance is a biologically based action, and every action has an equal and opposite reaction.

Every Action Has an Equal and Opposite Reaction

When an officer goes off duty, the sympathetic branch of the autonomic nervous system, which controls on-duty reactions necessary for survival, gives way to the parasympathetic branch, which controls off-duty reactions. The alert, alive, engaged, quick-thinking individual changes into a detached, withdrawn, tired, and apathetic individual in his or her personal life. Every action has an equal and opposite reaction. *Biological homeostasis*, which is the biological balancing phenomena, turns the person who has been experiencing the hypervigilance reaction on duty into the person experiencing the direct opposite reaction off duty.

Every Action Has an Equal and Opposite Reaction

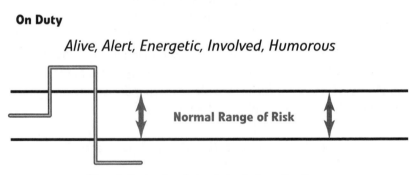

On Duty

Alive, Alert, Energetic, Involved, Humorous

Normal Range of Risk

Tired, Detached, Isolated, Apathetic

Off Duty

This officer, or "heat seeker," who experiences energy, stimulation, and social interaction and involvement while on duty can turn into the off-duty couch potato. The working officer who socially engages other individuals and practices alert and alive officer safety skills while on duty can have trouble responding to a normal conversation at home. The friend, spouse, or significant other who describes the police officer companion during the off-duty phase of life often makes these observations:

> *The working officer who socially engages other individuals and practices alert and alive officer safety skills while on duty can have trouble responding to a normal conversation at home.*

 "She is different now that she's a cop."

"He never talks anymore."

"He comes home, sits in front of the TV, and tunes out the world."

"She won't even answer the telephone."

"When we are out driving, he just looks out the window and says nothing."

The significant other in the officer's life is describing the lower phase of the hypervigilance cycle. "She's different now"—yes, all officers are different. They are experiencing hypervigilance and in many ways live in two different biological worlds. One is typified by alertness, involvement, aliveness, and social engagement, while the other world, at home, is typified by exhaustion, isolation, apathy, and on occasion, unfortunately, anger.

On Duty **Heat Seeker** *(Sympathetic branch)*	Off Duty **Couch Potato** *(Parasympathetic branch)*
Alert	Tired
Alive	Isolated
Quick thinking	Detached
Good sense of humor	Apathetic
Camaraderie	Angry

What is taking place is a swing between the two aspects of hypervigilance, the on-duty and off-duty phases. Because every action has an equal and opposite reaction, the high demand for more elevated alertness that is required for on-duty police work will produce, unless corrected, an extreme reaction in the opposite direction when off duty. This pendulum-like swing occurs daily in the officer's life. The swings can be conceptualized as a rollercoaster: highs when in the police role followed by lows in the personal role.

Because every action has an equal and opposite reaction, the high demand for more elevated alertness that is required for on-duty police work will produce, unless corrected, an extreme reaction in the opposite direction when off duty.

Many officers and spouses have not been trained in the hypervigilance biological rollercoaster and they find their relationship strained, even broken, by the pendulous swing from alertness at work to indifference at home.

The Hypervigilance Biological Rollercoaster

6

What happens to law enforcement officers who move every day between the two different biological worlds of on-duty and off-duty functioning? What are the obstacles officers must overcome to create balanced lives between the two phases of the hypervigilance reaction?

The biological rollercoaster created by hypervigilance can take over the day-to-day lives of police officers and their families and destroy the fabric of their lives. The capacity to picture the rollercoaster is essential to understanding the dynamics taking place at work and at home and to learn strategies to break the destructive effect the rollercoaster can produce on police officers and their families.

Hypervigilance keeps officers alive on the street, but they return home to a state that is the opposite of hypervigilance. Without awareness of the effects of the rollercoaster, an officer's life can become controlled by this pendulous effect. If not mastered, the rollercoaster can become the major force in shaping an officer's life. The down side of the rollercoaster can, without the officer's awareness of its destructive effects, begin determining non-police-related activities and relationships. What is it like for the officer returning home to the down side of the hypervigilance cycle? The up side has a physically pleasant feeling, but the opposite is true of the down side. The following descriptions of officer behavior while off duty tell the story:

" *"I know when he's sitting in front of the TV and I'm talking to him, he doesn't hear a word of what I'm saying."*

—an officer's wife

"We drove upstate last week to visit my folks. She looked out the window and all I got were one-word answers. Then all of a sudden a car sped by us and she said, 'Why don't I see those assholes when I'm on duty?' "

—an officer's husband

"The only time she says anything at all is when it has something to do with work."

—an officer's son

"He doesn't hardly speak to me, but when someone from work calls on the telephone he's back alive, full of emotion, questions, and conversation about work. But then when he hangs up the phone and I ask 'Who was that on the telephone?' all I get is a distant 'Ah, nobody really.' "

—an officer's significant other

"When I come home after work, even though I've been looking forward all day to getting home and seeing my family, I walk through the door and it hits me. I feel drugged. All I want to do is be left alone."

—an officer

"I can sit in front of the TV and surf channels every five seconds and just veg out for hours on end."

—an officer

This two-phase effect of hypervigilance on the life of a law enforcement officer can create challenges to maintaining a balanced personal life. If the challenges are not successfully met or the Hypervigilance Biological Rollercoaster® is not understood, relationships fail, inappropriate behavior increases, and lives can be irreparably broken. Officers who do not understand the up-and-down nature of the rollercoaster only know that they feel more "normal" at work, more "alive" at work. They know that when they walk through the doors to their homes and personal lives, they can feel like zombies who don't talk and don't want to do anything—unfortunately, the families don't know why.

Recovery from the Rollercoaster

Because the hypervigilance rollercoaster is a biological cycle, it will actually self-correct if left alone. For example, after approximately eighteen to twenty-four hours, the effects of hypervigilance will be alleviated and the person will return to a normal phase of social inter-action, emotion, and perception.

The Hypervigilance Recovery Period

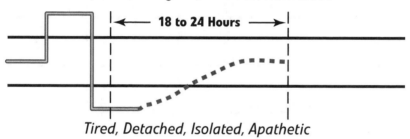

This recovery period raises one very important question, however, for the average police officer:

"What do you typically do within eighteen to twenty-four hours after you return home from work?"

There are several possible responses, such as eat, sleep, or visit with family and friends, but the overriding response in terms of importance and potential impact on the hypervigilance rollercoaster is this:

"Go back to work."

The officer returns to the on-duty world of required safety-based perception, back to the world of hypervigilance. What this creates is a lifestyle based on the swings between the extremes of perceptual alertness caused by the necessity to be hypervigilant on the streets and the opposite reaction of extreme detachment and inactivity at home. This swing becomes the everyday life of the police officer and also of the police family.

The Hypervigilance Biological Rollercoaster®

On Duty

Alive, Alert, Energetic, Involved, Humorous

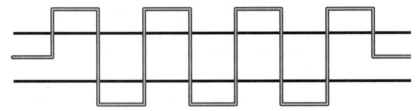

Tired, Detached, Isolated, Apathetic

Off Duty

Two extremes exist every day in the life of a police officer. The problem is, if the officer and family are not aware of the cycle and its potential destruction, they can't be expected to take the appropriate corrective action and avoid the devastating effects on both their personal and professional lives. This day-to-day cycle of high elevation at work followed by detachment, social isolation, and exhaustion at home redefines the daily pattern for many police officers. It also means very little time is spent within the normal range or between the lines—*maybe* an officer will hit the normal range while traveling to and from work. The officer now actually exists in two worlds, with what appear to be two lives: the on-duty police life and the off-duty personal life. Not to be informed of the rollercoaster keeps the officer and family in the dark about what is taking place, what they can do to break this destructive cycle, and how they can do it.

> *This day-to-day cycle of high elevation at work followed by detachment, social isolation, and exhaustion at home redefines the daily pattern for many police officers.*

The Magic Chair

In many occupational fields, the workforce returns home exhausted and disengaged from friends or family. The majority of these occupational fields, however, see the worker come home exhausted from a long day of physically demanding and sometimes backbreaking labor. The officer also is exhausted—not from having expended extreme amounts of muscular energy, but from the effects of heightened awareness, the effects of hypervigilance. The officer is physically exhausted because the hypervigilance cycle is biological, not psychological. Many officers unaware of the rollercoaster come home and fall into a classic dilemma that haunts many police families: the "magic chair."

Most police officers, male or female, single or married, have magic chairs. They don't call them by that name but, nonetheless, they possess them and use them on an almost daily basis. These are called magic chairs because as soon as officers sit in them, after returning home from work, by "magic" all their blood instantly turns into lead. They can't talk, they can't answer even the most basic question asked by a family member—all they can do is sit and enter into a vegetative off-duty phase. Most frequently the magic chair is operated in conjunction with an electronic device for enhanced effect, typically a television set, preferably one with multichannel cable or satellite capacity.

Here's how it works: The officer approaches the chair, sits in it, and makes some form of ritualistic verbalization: for example, "what a day." This is followed by reaching for the remote control and switching on the television set. The lower half of the biological rollercoaster is now in operation. All the biological attributes that typified the on-duty, upper reaches of the rollercoaster, such as peripheral vision, acute hearing, rapid thinking, and decision making, are all unnecessary now that survival is no longer at risk—the reverse effects take place. The on-duty attributes are soon replaced by the off-duty attributes until the officer is riding the magic chair to full effect. He or she sees nothing but the television set because tunnel vision has taken over. The officer hears nothing but what is being said on the television. Everybody and everything else is blocked out. How long does the officer watch each channel for? About three to five seconds, on average. This channel changing demonstrates that it is not the content of the program being viewed that is controlling the focused behavior, just the process of "checking out," detaching from the surrounding environment. This is the direct opposite response from that of the on-duty phase.

The officer is using the magic chair to recover while in the bottom half of the rollercoaster. How long can the average officer remain in the lower phase, switching channels on the television every three to five seconds? Ask officers and many will say something like this:

"Until I fall asleep."

"Eighteen to twenty-four hours, and then I have to go back to work."

Typically, sitting in the magic chair is not in itself a problem. It does not cause any known injury to vital organs or functions. It could, however, be considered a major problem if the officer resides with another life form. This could be a wife, husband, significant other, child, or even a pet cat or dog. The other life form might want to do something "outrageous," like talk. What happens when the other person attempts to transmit a communication to the officer now in the magic chair? It soon becomes very clear that the person is transmitting, but the officer is not receiving. The officer has mastered the capacity to tune out. Officers may not know why or how they do it, but they do it very well. When in the magic chair and asked a question by a significant other in his or her personal life, the officer doesn't really hear the question but has mastered a unique communication style. She or he has mastered the art of the "nonsense transmission."

This is a verbal nonresponse to the person who, unfortunately, is attempting to engage the officer in a personal conversation. The nonsense transmission has no inherent content value as a message. It is a verbal utterance designed solely to keep the person from bothering the off-duty officer who is in magic chair mode.

Nonsense Transmissions

Typical examples of nonsense transmissions:

- "Sure, babe, we'll talk about it later."
- "Whatever you think is fine with me."
- "Why don't you kids go outside and play? I'll look at your homework a little later."
- "Sure, that sounds good."
- "Sure, we'll see."
- "Yeah, maybe."

The nonsense transmission is designed to keep the other person at arm's length and give the appearance of social interaction without being overtly offensive toward the party wishing to interact. The officer hears nothing and sees nothing, which is a very effective form of sensory blockage. It is biologically based but can be corrected if the officer and significant others know of its existence. If they don't know of its existence, hard feelings, rejection, social isolation, and failed relationships can be the consequences.

Magic Chair Test

Anyone in a relationship with a police officer can test for the magic chair phenomena by taking the following steps:

Once you believe the off-duty officer is in the magic chair, engaged in staring at the television set and tuning out the world, begin the test by starting an insignificant conversation while standing approximately six to ten feet to the right or left of the officer. As you transmit statements or questions and receive nonsense transmissions in return, quietly begin moving closer and closer to the officer, until you are standing between the officer and the television set, blocking his or her view of the television.

If the officer says something like, "Come on, honey, step aside. I'm trying to watch this," then the officer doesn't have the condition in an extreme form because he or she is actually acknowledging your presence by interacting with you. If the officer reaches up and gently guides you aside to see the television, the condition is not extreme because he or she is validating your presence by touching you, acknowledging your existence.

If, however, when you quietly step in front of the officer, blocking the view of the television set, and his or her brain goes on auto-pilot, the unconscious correction mode, and the officer slightly leans to the left or right to look around you without saying a word, the condition exists in an extreme form and warning bells should go off to address the issue before the relationship suffers harm.

The magic chair comes in various modes:
- "I'm watching television" mode
- "I'm on the computer" mode
- "I'm reading the newspaper" mode
- "I'm taking a nap" mode
- "I'm just thinking about something" mode

Although it can appear, at first glance, to be a normal, benign form of recovery after a hard day's work, the magic chair phenomenon can start a process of deterioration in the quality of relationships between the police officer and those persons central to his or her personal life. What happens when the lower phase of the rollercoaster becomes the normal way of interacting at home? The relationship stops having the level of emotional energy invested in it that is required to maintain a dynamic, growing relationship. Nothing drastic happens at first; however, gradual erosion is taking place. The family has fewer conversations and spends less time together. When this phenomenon is compounded with the effects of long hours, rotating shift work, and, possibly, moonlighting at an off-duty job, the consequences can begin to destroy even the most solid relationship.

Mistaking the Rollercoaster for Other Problems
Unless officers act to change the lower phase of the cycle, their personal lives will change. If a mental health professional looked at the lower phase of the hypervigilance cycle, noting the isolation, apathy, detachment, and exhaustion, the professional would probably describe the state as depression. Although the lower phase of the Hypervigilance Biological Rollercoaster® produces many aspects similar to depression, it is not true clinical depression. True depression does not involve the rapid thinking processes, social engagement, quick wit, and independent decision making that typifies the on-duty phase of the officer's life. All the mental health professional would need to see is the on-duty phase of the same officer to realize it is not depression that is taking place but rather some type of cyclical change. If this swing of emotional energy could confuse the mental health professional, what about the individual officers and those with whom they share personal lives?

Wouldn't they also be confused? Compound the confusion about what is taking place by adding shift work to the equation and many relationships become extremely strained.

Why?

The often-heard "why" questions asked by the significant others in an officer's life show the confusion created by the rollercoaster:

- "Why doesn't he talk anymore when he comes home?"
- "Why don't we do anything anymore?"
- "Why don't we have the 'up' times like we used to have?"
- "Why don't we go anywhere anymore?"
- "Why is everything so negative when she talks?"
- "Why when we are in the car does he just stare out the window and not say anything?"
- "Why isn't she ever at home anymore?"

Without insight into what is taking place, not only are the significant others asking questions about what is going on, the officers also are attempting to explain to themselves what they are experiencing. Why do they feel one way at work and another way at home? Some officers, without benefit of information concerning the rollercoaster, come home and experience the down side of the hypervigilance effect and do not understand this emotional elevator drop. They walk through the door and feel tired, disinterested, detached, and, unfortunately, they form incorrect conclusions. Without knowing what is taking place in their lives, they mistakenly conclude that the people and events in their personal lives are actually causing the change in feelings they are experiencing. They have not been informed that the emotional changes they are experiencing are part of

> *They have not been informed that the emotional changes they are experiencing are part of a predictable biological process that is taking place inside them and is not being caused by the people in their lives.*

a predictable biological process that is taking place *inside them* and is not being caused by the people in their lives. Without this knowledge of the impact of hypervigilance, officers can draw incorrect and damaging conclusions that can have devastating long-term effects on their personal lives. The hypervigilance rollercoaster may have visible social and psychological consequences, but the root causes are biological in nature.

It Must Be Their Fault

Without knowing that the emotional and perceptual swing is something taking place biologically within them, officers can mistakenly project responsibility for their emotions onto the home and those in their personal lives:

> *"I guess I love my family, but I really can't stand being there. I walk into the house and realize, man, I don't want to be here. It's not something I can put my finger on. I'm just not happy at home. I get angry at everything, and in my mind nobody can do anything right. I just want to be left alone. At home they really make me crazy."*

Many officers experience the down cycle repeatedly and they don't know how to solve the issue because they don't know what is taking place. They only know that they feel one way at work and the opposite at home. Work is a fun place where they feel alive and have lots to do and get involved with; home, on the other hand, is boring.

> *"I'm tired and the last thing I want to do is sit and talk."*

The officers who do not have good emotional survival training in how to break this cycle may practice good street survival skills while at work, but then go home and collapse. They experience this cycle each day and cannot identify what is taking place. They have not been informed of the biological flip side of officer safety. The just know the cycle from living it each day.

The Cycle

Go to work, get off duty, go home, get depressed. . . . Go to work, get off duty, go home, get depressed. . . . Go to work, get off duty, go home, get depressed. . . . Go to work, get off duty, go home, get depressed. . . . Go to work, get off duty, go home, get depressed.

How do you break this cycle? Mistakenly, most officers decide:

"Don't go home."

This mistaken conclusion by officers has probably caused more heartache and destruction in police families than all the felons' bullets ever fired.

Don't Go Home

"Don't go home" can become an unconscious way of breaking the cycle. At first, it is not a conscious way of avoiding home as much as a conscious awareness that while on duty the world is alive, stimulating, and invigorating, and off duty, at home, it is subdued, depressing, and isolating.

How do officers not go home? Stay at work for long hours. Overtime is very much rewarded in the police culture. Unenlightened supervisors and managers can mistakenly confuse this behavior as a high degree of commitment to the police career, which it is in the short run, but clearly this extra work has destructive long-term consequences both personally and professionally.

Another way of not going home is stopping after work with fellow officers and having a few drinks, sometimes referred to as the traditional "choir practice." It's an attempt to ward off the emotional drop that hits when the officer moves from the on-duty phase of hypervigilance to the off-duty phase. Socializing with fellow officers and families can be an appropriate and healthy activity—if done within reason. However, this is often a fertile ground for inappropriate and high-risk behaviors that can jeopardize the officer personally and professionally. How many choir practices have become launching pads for broken marriages? How many careers and, tragically, lives have ended due to impaired driving and DUI arrests during the officer's journey home?

Another way of not going home can be working off-duty jobs, or "detail work." For many officers, off-duty employment has a twofold effect. It clearly assists the family's financial needs but also lets the officer remain in the more alive mode of the officer role. She or he doesn't have to develop other, more constructive strategies or skills for breaking the rollercoaster effect. Although the willingness to do the off-duty or detail work is rooted partly in a well-internalized and commendable work ethic, no matter how noble the cause, "not going home" is the end result.

Disengage

Ask police officers what they enjoy doing after they return home and many give a very simple response:

- "Nothing."
- "Kicking back."
- "Relaxing."
- "Vegging out."

What does this disengagement from the nonpolice role of the officer's life look like in terms of the hypervigilance rollercoaster? See the figure below.

The Hypervigilance Biological Rollercoaster®: Disengagement from Personal Life

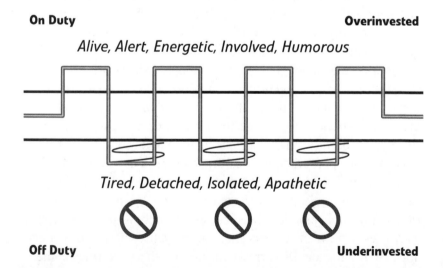

On Duty   **Overinvested**

Alive, Alert, Energetic, Involved, Humorous

Tired, Detached, Isolated, Apathetic

Off Duty   **Underinvested**

Many times the officer basically stops engaging in activities during the lower phase of her or his life. The slashes in the lower phase of the diagram above indicate that off-duty activities can cease to exist as a significant aspect of the officer's life. Officers become significantly *underinvested emotionally* in the personal aspects of their lives. Conversely, they become *overinvested emotionally* in the police role phase of their lives. This imbalance, which starts off as naive rookie enthusiasm, can become a damaging situation of being emotionally overinvested in the police role and can create destruction along multiple dimensions of officers' lives. The obvious first dimension to be affected is in an officer's personal life. All aspects of the officer's personal life can become associated with or "tainted" by the lower phase of the cycle. Everything to do with work is associated with the upper phase.

> *The lower phase, or off-duty life, of the officer tragically becomes of secondary importance.*

The lower phase, or off-duty life, of the officer tragically becomes of secondary importance. Unfortunately, so do many of the people who play emotional roles in the personal life of the officer.

Symptoms of the Hypervigilance Rollercoaster

How does an officer know if she or he is falling victim to the hypervigilance cycle and its effects of home avoidance and work overinvestment?

If an officer or significant other is trying to determine the effect of the rollercoaster on their relationship, each should know the symptoms. Following are the first warning signs or symptoms that an officer is falling victim to the hypervigilance rollercoaster. (See chapter 8 for corrective strategies and ways to address the lower phases of the rollercoaster and maintain a balanced emotional perspective.)

1. The desire for social isolation at home: Officers can find themselves being noncommunicative, withdrawn, and apathetic concerning family activities. Officers assume their domestic partner will take care of "all the mundane activities" such as raising kids, maintaining the home, and having a personal life. This is demonstrated by the officer riding the magic chair after spending an on-duty day as a heat seeker.

2. Unwillingness to engage in conversation or activities that are not police related: This effect is obvious to any observer at a police social encounter. Go to the party and notice how the conversation revolves around "war stories." One of the reasons for this type of social interaction is that as each verbal exchange takes place, and each story is told, the officers listening to the war story vicariously experience the physiological reaction of returning to hypervigilance. Telling war stories and socializing with other officers gets the blood flowing. It has tremendous antidepressant effects. It moves the people, both those telling the war stories and those listening, back up to the upper phase of the rollercoaster by producing short-term physical stimulation.

Officers assume their domestic partner will take care of "all the mundane activities" such as raising kids, maintaining the home, and having a personal life.

It feels good to tell war stories in the earlier years of a law enforcement career. The socialization process by which officers interact by taking turns telling war stories is called *adrenal masturbation*—it has exciting short-term physical consequences but is totally nonproductive.

3. Reduced interaction with nonpolice friends and acquaintances: Officers spend their time with other officers. Squad parties, choir practices, and other social encounters revolving around work become the socialization pattern to the exclusion of old friends. Often officers will rationalize the closed social network of primarily socializing with other officers: "I get tired of these other people. Once they find out you're a cop, all they want to do is complain about some ticket they got or something. I don't want to talk about work." Actually this particular rationalization or excuse is the direct opposite of reality. One of the reasons cops, particularly young cops, don't like to talk or socialize with friends who are not in police work is, "those other folks don't have any good stories." They live pretty mundane, boring lives. The nonpolice friends live "between the lines." They don't have any great war stories to tell. Picture an interaction between an officer of two or three years in law enforcement and an old nonpolice friend who sells fencing material.

The friend relates, "John, I just sold 8,500 feet of chain link fence to the school district."

The officer thinks, "So what? Who gives a damn."

Only the feeling of being on the upper level of the hypervigilance rollercoaster, either at work or while socializing, validates a feeling of aliveness or self-worth for the officer. Everything else is boring.

4. Procrastination in decision making not related to work. Officers can begin withdrawing from decision making and any self-initiated off-duty activities. An example of this is in the following case history.

This example concerns a highly active police officer who has no trouble making very complex decisions during the course of the work day. He routinely makes complex decisions concerning tactical issues and search-and-seizure questions. In addition to his full-time assignment, he also functions as an operations supervisor for his agency's SWAT team.

One day, while en route home from work, the officer receives a pager message from his spouse asking him to stop and pick up some groceries. The officer enters the store approximately twenty minutes after getting off duty and he walks right past me (a coworker of many years) and does not recognize me. After shopping, the officer gets in the line to check out his groceries, giving an external impression of "doing the zombie shop." He puts the groceries on the conveyor belt and the clerk scans the groceries and engages the officer in the following conversation:

Clerk:	*Good evening, sir.*
Officer:	*[inaudible grunt]*
Clerk:	*How are you tonight, sir?*
Officer:	*[second inaudible grunt]*
Clerk:	*What will that be tonight, sir, paper or plastic?*
Officer:	*[third inaudible grunt]*
Clerk:	*What will that be tonight, sir, paper or plastic?*
Officer:	*[Heavy sigh, hesitation] Surprise me.*

Obviously, "surprise me" isn't an answer, it's an abdication of an answer. It is an abandoning of any responsibility to make a decision. The officer is probably rationalizing his nonanswer with some thoughts along the lines of "who gives a shit" (a very common police rationalization for noninvolvement in decision making and nonparticipation in non-police-related activities)—it was just a grocery bag. If this type of nonparticipation or procrastination in decision making were used only in situations of the magnitude of "paper or plastic," it would not pose a difficulty in the officer's personal life. Unfortunately, however, even in major decisions that police families are required to make on a day-to-day basis, the officer member many times is not present, participating, or involved. As one police spouse answered a question I posed:

Author: *How many children do you have?*
Police spouse: *Counting my husband?*

Author: *Counting your husband, what do you mean?*
Police spouse: *Well, he's like another child. I mean, if we're*
                  going on a trip or something, I have to pack for
                  the kids and then I have to pack for him.
                  Otherwise he doesn't bring anything and com-
                  plains because he doesn't have any clothes or
                  anything. It's easier just to count him as one of
                  the kids.

It might be easier in the short run "to count him as one of the kids," but what impact on the relationship does this abdication of responsibility have on any sense of adult partnership?

> *"I've been making decisions all week. Whatever you want*
> *is fine with me."*

This statement, along with the paper or plastic dilemma, illustrates how many officers can make wonderful decisions while functioning in the upper phase of the hypervigilance rollercoaster, but cannot or do not want to make even the most basic decisions while in the lower phases.

This withdrawal from decision making can leave the spouse or significant other with a sense of abandonment and, on occasion, a feeling of being overwhelmed by the responsibility of running the household on his or her own. One spouse told of her officer-husband who heard on the evening news that mortgage rates were falling and announced to his spouse: "Honey, why don't you take care of refinancing the house and see what kind of a new mortgage we can get." The idea of making a joint decision on the mortgage was not even spoken of—only the concept "you handle it, I got stuff at work to do." This withdrawal from involvement in one's own personal life has major implications in the overall functioning in both the officer's personal and professional realms.

This withdrawal from decision making can leave the spouse or significant other with a sense of abandonment and, on occasion, a feeling of being overwhelmed by the responsibility of running the household on his or her own.

5. Infidelity: This is one of the most painful aspects of the hypervigilance rollercoaster. Anything associated with "home" or the lower phase of the rollercoaster is boring, and anything associated with the upper phase is exciting, stimulating, and dynamic. Without insight or training in the effects of the rollercoaster, relationships shatter. People meeting and interacting during the upper phases appear brighter, wittier, prettier, more handsome—"the reds are redder and the blues are bluer." Emotions surge and individuals, particularly those experiencing the strain caused by the rollercoaster in their personal lives, find a terribly destructive way not to go home—they go to someone else's home. Infidelity begins with the surging emotions shared at the upper phase of the rollercoaster. People bond when they share risk. This has always accounted for the close relationships among police officers. It has become more complex, as has the overall workplace, with both genders represented in more equal proportions in recent years. The failure of some marriages and relationships are readily understandable to an outside observer who knew the relationship; however, some relationship failures defy a strictly logical explanation when one sees the new individual with whom the officer has become involved. Case histories point out the painful consequences and total bewilderment that can be experienced by the partner left behind by new relationships that, many times, are superficially initiated and based only on time shared in the upper phase of the rollercoaster.

Case History

Police Spouse: I don't know why she is doing this. I think I have been very supportive of her. I did all the work here at home while she went to the police academy. I took care of the kids and did all the housework, in addition to my own job, which is never just forty hours a week. Is it something I did? What can I do to win her back? I try to understand and be supportive of her police work. I think I really am. I wasn't wild about her going into the police department, but it was something she wanted to do. She's my life partner, so I supported her decision. I helped her in the academy with her notebooks and typing. I know it was real hard physically for her and she was always tired, so I made sure I helped. I retyped her class notes each day. I shined her leather for inspections—heck, I was in the Marines and I think I actually spit-shined her boots and leather every night after she went to sleep, so she could get eight hours of rest. I would do anything to get her back. I think she's totally forgotten about me and the kids. She started running around with one of the cops she works with and, hell, he's married, and I guess it's breaking up that marriage, too. I don't know what changed her thinking. We've been together for twelve years and I thought something like this would never happen to us.

Case History

Police Spouse: I don't know why he wants to end the marriage. I know I have gained some weight since we got married, but not that much. I've had two babies. I try to look pretty for him. If he's interested in being physical, I try to never turn him away, even when he comes home at those oddball hours in the middle of the night. I don't know what he sees in her. She's a waitress at the café all the cops hang out at. I know she's been going to the squad parties, one of the other wives told me. I can't see him giving up his family, the kids, the house, and the marriage for her. I mean she's nothing to look at, and I hear her kids are already in trouble with the law. Her ex-husband has been in prison. I don't understand what has gotten into him. He has always been so level headed. I can't explain how our whole world fell apart so fast.

The loss of solid police families can be due to superficial relationships, the foundations of which are based only on time shared in the upper phase of the rollercoaster. These relationships tend to be rapidly forming, intense, and many times typified by abrupt changes in the behavior of the officer, such as abandoning her or his marriage or existing relationship. The new relationship, many times, has elements that resemble an adolescent's running away from home. Officers leaving the previously existing relationship often feel extreme guilt; however, they simultaneously feel a tremendous sense of freedom and aliveness to be out of the existing relationship or marriage. They may have tragically formed the wrong conclusion and believed the existing marriage or relationship itself was the source of their unfulfilled feelings and depression. They can form the conclusion that it was membership in the relationship or marriage that was causing the depressed or empty feeling at home. The reality, in many cases, is that it was the effects of the hypervigilance rollercoaster taking a destructive toll on the law enforcement officer and the people in his or her personal life.

6. Noninvolvement in children's needs and activities. In many law enforcement families, children interact with the officer parent only in the lower reaches of the rollercoaster. Several case histories can demonstrate this.

Case History

A forty-two-year-old narcotics sergeant calls me from a jurisdiction approximately 150 miles away and asks if he can have an appointment to discuss a criminal profiling question. I inquire if the information can be discussed on the telephone, saving the sergeant an approximately three-hour drive to my office. The sergeant is more than willing to drive the three hours and relates he would feel more comfortable discussing the case in person. So we make the appointment and the sergeant arrives for his scheduled meeting.

After approximately twenty-five minutes of discussing the criminal profiling question, the sergeant stands, prepares to leave my office, and states, "Well, I guess that means it's over?" I assume the sergeant means the appointment to discuss the criminal profiling case and reply, "No, if you think we need more time, I have the next

(continued)

two hours open," whereupon the sergeant begins crying and says, "No, I mean I guess that means his childhood is over." I am caught totally unprepared for the sergeant's statement and the emotional reaction that seems totally outside the context of the criminal profiling discussion.

I ask, "What's going on?" The sergeant tearfully relates, "I guess that means his childhood is over. I always thought I was going to be the kind of father that did things with his kids, you know, went camping and hiking and took them to baseball games. Well, it really hit me hard about two weeks ago. My youngest son, who is eighteen, just went into the Marine Corps. He left for bootcamp and it really hit me hard. I have three kids and I never did any of those things with them. I always thought I would, but there was always another dope deal to work or another search warrant to do. I have been breaking down crying since he left at the airport. My wife says 'Honey, it will be OK, it's just his time to go and do the things in life he wants to do; it will be OK.' I can't figure it out. She's doing OK and I'm breaking down crying now for two weeks. It's not that I just miss my boy, it's that I realize I missed his childhood. I think my wife is doing better with this than me because she did all those things with him. She was the Cub Scout mom, the soccer mom, hell, she was always doing stuff with all three of the kids and worked full-time besides. I never did shit with the kids. I love them, but I guess you have to show it with your actions not with just what you feel inside. You have to put those feelings into action. I wish I could do it all over again!"

Case History

I am instructing a class at a large police department in an eastern state when a young police officer approaches me during a class break, immediately after a discussion of the hypervigilance rollercoaster. The young officer inquires, "Do you know how long I've known my father for?" I, not ever having met the officer before, am somewhat bewildered by the question and respond that I have no idea how long the officer has known his father.

The young officer responds, "Of course not," and continues, "I've known my father for five years—oh, don't get me wrong, I was raised in a home with my father present, but I never knew him. I met my father five years ago when I became a police officer. My father is a lieutenant on this department and when I arrived at the academy and people saw my last name on my name tag, all I heard was, 'You must be Lt._____'s son. Your dad is a hell of a guy.'

"I would hear about my dad from everybody I met. They would tell me about my dad and what they had done together. One cop tells me, 'I'll never forget your dad. The day my wife was in a terrible car accident, I was working on his squad. He spent the whole night and most of the next day with me waiting at the hospital until my wife was out of the woods. Your dad is one hell of a great guy. I'd do anything for him.'

"It wasn't until right now hearing you talk about that hypervigilance rollercoaster that I realized all those cops knew the man at the top half of the rollercoaster; growing up, I only knew the man at the bottom half of the rollercoaster. Since I became an officer, I see my father almost every day. Now we have a great relationship. We talk all the time, mostly about the department and everything, but then we talk about all kinds of other stuff. He comes over to my house and helps me with projects at my place and does stuff with my kids. I find myself over helping Mom and him on stuff around their house. Growing up, it wasn't that he did anything bad at home, he just never did anything. Cops should be taught about this rollercoaster so they can do what they have to do to make it right at home. I'm lucky I became a cop and got to know my father. My brothers are not cops and they probably don't see our father three times a year. All my brothers know is the man at the bottom of the rollercoaster. What a loss for police families when they don't learn this stuff until it is too late!"

7. The "I usta" syndrome—loss of interest in hobbies or recreational activities: To see the effects of the hypervigilance rollercoaster on off-duty activities, ask an officer to describe his or her personal life. When I inquire specifically about what officers like to do when they are not doing police work, I often receive an interesting set of responses:

Question: *Tell me a little about yourself.*
Officer's answer: *I work uniform patrol in the second shift. Been there about five years.*

Question:	*Do you like it?*
Officer's answer:	*Yeah, it's okay. You know the normal stuff, lots of calls. Yeah, I like it. I like being a cop here with this department.*
Question:	*What about your personal life?*
Officer's answer:	*Well, I'm married. My spouse works over at the hospital. We have two kids.*
Question:	*That's great. What do you like to do when you're not working, you know, hobbies or non-work-related activities?*
Officer's answer:	*I really like to go fishing. I am really into that. We got some great streams and lakes not far from here at all.*
Question:	*That's great! How often do you get out fishing?*
Officer's answer:	*I try to get out as often as I can.*
Question:	*That's great, but when was the last time you went fishing?*
Officer's answer:	*Oh, I don't know, it has been a while. Like I said, I like to get out as often as I can.*
Question:	*But when exactly was the last time you went fishing?*
Officer's answer:	*Exactly, boy, I don't know. You know we're real short in the field right now, and we're waiting for that academy class to graduate to put a few more people on the street.*
Question:	*Okay, but exactly when was the last time you went fishing?*
Officer's answer:	*Exactly? Oh, I don't know exactly, but like I said, we're real short of officers in the field. Exactly, I guess, I don't know maybe, exactly, to tell you the truth, I guess it's been about two years, but I usta go all the time.*

The "I usta" response is given by many law enforcement officers to describe any inquiry into their personal lives. It describes what they "used to" do before becoming police officers. The "I usta" syndrome is basically a statement that all those activities that existed before becoming a police officer, that helped define the officer as a complete person, have been put on the back burner. They are the activities that get lost because they occur at the bottom half of the rollercoaster.

"I Usta"

- "I usta fish."
- "I usta hunt."
- "I usta jog."
- "I usta sew."
- "I usta work out."
- "I usta go to church."
- "I usta go camping."
- "I usta see old friends."
- "I usta keep my house picked up and tidy."
- "I usta lay out my uniform the night before, so it looked sharp, and I'd shine my leather."
- "I usta do crafts and handiwork."
- "I usta take my kids to the park."
- "I usta read to my kids."
- "I usta visit my folks."
- "I usta lift weights."
- "I usta sing in the church choir."
- "I usta do woodworking."
- "I usta garden."

How many of the above sound familiar to you?

The "I usta" phase can deteriorate even further into more generalized senses of loss:

"I usta to be married."
"I usta to have a personal life."
"I usta to give a damn about this job."

The "I usta" syndrome is a description of the things that have been lost from the officer's life, the things that are not work related and that reside at the bottom of the rollercoaster. This is a lost part of life, the nonpolice personal life, the part where all the other nonwork, nonpolice aspects of life are experienced, such as family, hobbies, and interests. This is also the part of the police officer's life that provides the complete picture of the whole person. It is the phase that keeps officers' lives together and balanced through the trying times and tragic experiences that occur in every police career.

The "I usta" syndrome is the generalized effect of the hypervigilance rollercoaster on the personal interests and nonpolice behaviors of the officer. All the activities that defined the complete man or woman before he or she became a police officer can be lost. If these other parts of life are lost, a new person emerges, many times a new person without the balancing strengths of multiple dimensions, activities, or roles in life to draw upon for perspective and understanding. Without this balance, the short-term day-to-day effects of the hypervigilance rollercoaster begin to turn into long-term, more damaging losses.

> *The "I usta" syndrome is basically a statement that all those activities that existed before becoming a police officer, that helped define the officer as a complete person, have been put on the back burner.*

Long–Term Effects of Hypervigilance

Police training is designed to prepare officers to work the streets, to handle calls safely, and to practice good officer safety and street survival skills. That would be enough if officers were being asked to work the streets for only a few short years. A comparison of law enforcement with the military might help clarify the effects of long-term versus short-term exposure to a culture of risk.

Military versus Law Enforcement

The military also prepares people for total immersion into a culture of potential risk, knowing the majority of military personnel will spend an enlistment duration of four or so years on active duty and then leave the military for a return to civilian life. The military knows that it is a relatively short-term role for the individual to assume. Law enforcement organizations also train their personnel for total immersion into their own unique culture of potential risk, but unlike the military, every four or so years the vast majority of police officers do not leave. Most law enforcement officers see their occupational choice of law enforcement as a long-term professional career commitment, not something one moves out of after four years. Many officers would say, "You are just learning to be an effective cop after four years."

Most police agencies train new officers to be sprinters, and then they enter them into the marathon.

The training priorities and orientation of many law enforcement agencies produce enthusiastic rookies and, later, bitter and angry veterans. This process can be explained with an analogy: Most police agencies train new officers to be sprinters, and then they enter them into the marathon. The police career choice for many officers is a twenty-year or longer commitment. New officers start out highly enthusiastic, not able to get enough of police work; then, as the years go by, many officers go through some rather drastic changes in terms of how they view police work.

"I love this job."

changes to

"I hate this job and can't wait until I'm out of here."

Which Officers Are Most at Risk?

Who is most prone to experience the effects of the hypervigilance rollercoaster, the best law enforcement officers or the worst law enforcement officers? Clearly the answer is the best officers, the most dedicated, the most committed, the most highly motivated, the ones practicing the best hypervigilance and officer safety. These are the men and women who are dedicated to being the best possible officers they can be. Often, these women and men begin their career with only naive enthusiasm as a survival tactic for the emotional dimension of their lives. They are trained in how to handle the streets, they just aren't trained in how to handle the job and its effects on their personal lives.

If our best personnel are at highest risk of this phenomenon, who pays the price first? Who is the first victim of the hypervigilance rollercoaster? When I asked this question of a group of officers, one responded:

"That curve describes my life. You must be looking in my window, that's how I live. I have been a cop for eight years now and I really love it. I work in a part of town that really goes all the time. We run from call to call, but I really love it. I could transfer to a slower division, but I like working down here in this division where there is lots of activity, but when I get off-duty and go home, just like you say, I go through a mind melt. I want to be left alone. I sit in front of the TV. I don't say anything. I don't even answer the telephone if it rings. I let the answering machine get it. Your roller-coaster is exactly right in describing me."

At this point, I reiterated my question: "Thank you for your feedback on my concept of the hypervigilance model; however, the question that I asked was 'Who was the first victim?'"

The officer, after some reflection and thought, responded: "Well, the first victim, well, it's the first wife."

The female officers in the class concurred: "The first husband." Then one female officer responded by saying, "It is not the first husband or the first wife. If you're married it will affect your marriage, but this curve affects me and I'm not married, I've never been married, and, judging by the men I see at work each day, I assure you I'll never choose to get married. The first victim of this rollercoaster is your personal life."

Who Is the First Victim?

The officer is actually the first victim of the rollercoaster dynamic, although clearly many other people are affected by the loss of emotional and behavioral balance in an officer's life. As the number of non-police-related dimensions in officers' lives shrinks, officers are redefined. As the nonpolice aspects of officers' lives (or the things that they "usta" do) diminish, well-balanced individuals can be transformed into people who obtain the majority of their social and emotional needs from the police role. Everything else is put on the back burner or lost due to the "I usta" syndrome, which is brought on by the hypervigilance rollercoaster.

The nonpolice dimensions of officers' lives, such as spirituality, cultural and ethnic identification, core values, family, friends, hobbies, and other perceptual sets or ways of viewing the world, reduce if not disappear. The men and women who began their police career as bright, well-rounded, ethical officers begin experiencing major behavioral deficits in their personal lives. Because of the "I usta" syndrome, officers can begin distancing themselves from core aspects of their sense of self. The officer's identity becomes tied only to the police role.

Many people begin police work emotionally and socially well balanced. The highly selective employment requirements ideally screen out the emotionally and socially deficient from beginning a police career. The lower phase of the rollercoaster, however, causes officers to stop engaging in activities that are not police related when they're off duty. Some officers will reject this concept and say, "I went fishing last week," but if you probe further, you discover that, yes, the officer did go fishing last week, but he or she went with the squad. The question would need to be asked: Was it really a fishing trip? Or a choir practice with fishing poles? What was the main point of the trip? To relax and enjoy some activities with family and friends, or to spend time yet again in an ever tightening social group? A group that can unfortunately limit its interests solely to the happenings of police work and its individual police agency in particular.

The degree of emotional and social balance of individuals entering into law enforcement before the "I usta" syndrome takes place is graphically demonstrated below:

Before the "I Usta" Syndrome

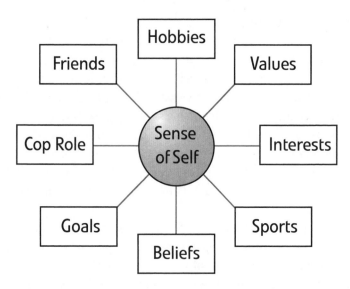

Those entering law enforcement have multiple dimensions in their lives, which add to their overall definition of themselves as complete people. They invest time and energy into numerous aspects of their lives, such as

- spirituality
- culture or ethnicity
- hobbies and interests
- friends
- family
- goals

Obviously, this list is not exhaustive. Each person has unique attributes that individually define her or him as a person. The emotional anchoring of multiple dimensions and support systems in a person's life determines his or her individual emotional stability and capacity to maintain perspective. As the young officer is exposed to the need to practice hypervigilance in order to survive the risks of the street, the rollercoaster takes effect and the nonpolice attributes, support systems, and other life dimensions shrink. The "I usta" syndrome can change the graphic on the opposite page into the one below:

After the "I Usta" Syndrome

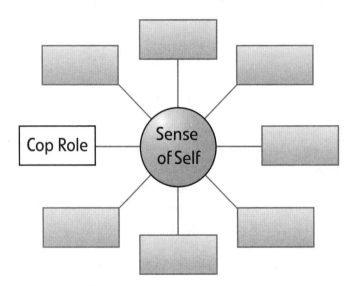

All other supporting dimensions or interests in the officer's life have basically disappeared. Officers who previously defined themselves by multiple aspects of their lives now define themselves by the singular dimension of their police role. They might still pay lip service to the other dimensions of their lives, the things they "usta" do, but the rollercoaster has created behavioral deficits in the number of areas or dimensions in which the officers are actually investing energy and time.

The sense of self is the sum total of all of the separate dimensions of the individual that combine to define him or her as a unique, free thinking, independent, and responsible person. The hypervigilance rollercoaster and the "I usta" syndrome clearly can have an impact on the sense of self of the individual who entered law enforcement and may cause significant emotional transformation during the journey from "the person" to "the officer." As behavioral activities of the off-duty phase of the rollercoaster continue to diminish, the sense of self continues to constrict. The broad-based sense of self at the time of entry into the field reduces to identification with only the police role.

Officers who previously defined themselves by multiple aspects of their lives now define themselves by the singular dimension of their police role.

Officers who have experienced this redefinition of their sense of self do not say:

"I work as a cop."

They say:

*"I **am** a cop."*

I Am a Cop

This can be an expression of significant and justifiable pride in being a law enforcement officer, or it can be an indication of significant *overidentification* with the police role and potentially a problematic perspective for the officer.

"I am a cop" defines the essential core of the sense of self for the officer.

"I am a cop" can transform a positive sense of pride in the professional role into an overshadowing of the other essential aspects of the officer's life and identity (or sense of self). It can create a significant *underidentification* with other life roles that balance each other and the cop role.

Roles that Can Balance the Cop Role

The following are examples of roles that an officer can underidentify with as a result of overidentifying with the cop role.

"I am a friend."
"I am a mother/father."
"I am a husband/wife."
"I am a church/synagogue member."
"I am a bowler."
"I am a hunter."
"I am an embroiderer."
"I am a gardener."
"I am a golfer."
"I am a mountain biker."

The loss of nonpolice dimensions in an officer's life due to the lower phase of the rollercoaster can, in one sweep of the brush, cause the woman or man to begin having emotional and personal difficulties at the beginning of her or his career. Progressing across the span of a law enforcement career, this reduction of the sense of self can produce an emotionally fragile individual. The officer's identity has been reduced from the previously broad-based sense of self to a sense of self with only one dimension:

"I am a cop."

The effects of this overidentification emotionally with the police role and the reducing of the sense of self to one dimension have significant impact on the personal and work relationships of the officer in numerous ways. As the officer's sense of self becomes increasingly one-dimensional, the officer becomes more at risk emotionally.

Who's in Control?

What would appear as an intense sense of pride in the profession of police work actually makes the officer significantly more fragile emotionally for a few reasons: One reason is that the "I usta" syndrome has reduced the number of available emotional support systems for the officer to rely upon, if needed. A second reason stems from a very basic concept of human autonomy:

Who controls the type of person you are?

Functional and healthy human beings maintain some control over their sense of self. They believe they have a degree of autonomy over their existence and have a major say in the events affecting their lives. People need to believe they have a significant degree of control over their own day-to-day existence, a sense of predictability to most major events affecting their lives. This sense of control is a core element in creating a sense of emotional equilibrium or stability. The greater the degree of control or autonomy an individual has in her or his life, the greater the degree of empowerment, stability, and autonomy she or he will experience emotionally. Stress or psychological dysfunction itself, many times, can be defined as the presence of low control in a person's life. Any situation that reduces the individual's degree of control in his or her own life can precipitate a sense of psychological distress. If the loss of control is combined with high demands the individual must handle, the degree of psychological imbalance or stress can be extremely high.

> *People need to believe they have a significant degree of control over their own day-to-day existence, a sense of predictability to most major events affecting their lives.*

Psychological dysfunction has two components:

High Demands
+
Low Control

As predictability, autonomy, and control of the sense of self decrease in a person's life, a sense of emotional vulnerability, susceptibility, and risk increase. As police officers decrease the number of dimensions or roles defining their sense of self and become increasingly invested in only the police role, they increase their level of emotional vulnerability.

A Sense of Singular Identity

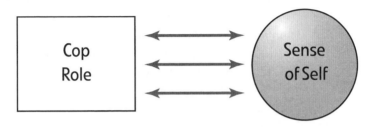

The officer's sense of self is defined by the singular role of being an officer. The sense of self and the job role have become welded together and are basically inseparable: "I *am* a cop." If having a sense of autonomy and a degree of control over the events affecting one's life is essential for an emotionally healthy individual, how does the over-identification with the police role affect the officer? The easiest way to explain how overidentification with the police role can destroy an emotionally healthy individual is to demonstrate the concept of the need to have autonomy or control in one's life. As an officer's sense of self becomes increasingly linked to the police role, who controls his or her police role? Ask officers this question:

"Who decides what kind of cop you're going to be?"

I've asked this question of large numbers of police officers for many years, and their answer is always the same:

"I do. I decide what kind of cop I am going to be."

At first glance, this response may appear to be an expression of emotional autonomy or self-responsibility. It would appear to be a sign of emotionally healthy, responsible individuals who see themselves in charge of their own behavior and who are willing to take responsibility for their own actions. The question and its response, however, are double-edged swords. The following exchange with a homicide detective demonstrates the potential dilemma.

Detective: *I decide what kind of cop I am going to be; it is up to me. I'm a homicide detective. I am very good at being a homicide detective. I've worked homicide for over eight years. I've testified in well over one hundred homicide cases. I'm an expert in several aspects of homicide investigation. I've attended many specialized schools on death investigation. I get a significant sense of satisfaction out of working as a homicide detective. I take pride in my job, and it is up to me to control my role and decide what kind of a homicide detective I am going to be.*

Initially, the homicide detective's response appears to demonstrate an individual who is willing to take responsibility for his own behavior, a core element of emotionally stable individuals. The potential emotional vulnerability and at-risk situation of this detective can be demonstrated by asking a few straightforward questions.

Author: *Sounds like you're a real competent homicide detective and take a great deal of pride in the job you do. It is a very necessary job, and I'm sure you get a sense of purpose, pride, and accomplishment from the job. Let me ask you, though, could you be approached right now by some boss from your agency, some high ranking person, a chief, a commander, or someone higher on the food chain than you, could they walk up to you and tap you on the shoulder and make you a non-homicide detective? Could they transfer you to a different investigations section or, even worse, back to uniform patrol?*

Detective: *Yeah, the boss could do all that to me in a New York minute.*

Author: *I'm confused. You just told me you decide what kind of homicide detective you are going to be. Now you say that the boss is the one who decides. Which is it? Do you decide or does the boss decide your role as a homicide detective?*

This interchange demonstrates the clear emotional vulnerability of the competent, dedicated police officer who has become emotionally vulnerable by having a one-dimensional sense of self, of overidentifying with the cop role, a role that consists of several dimensions that the officer clearly does not control.

Officers do not control many of the core issues of their jobs. They do not control many of the central aspects of the cop role. If the cop role and the sense of self have become identical, then the officer does not control her or his sense of self. This creates a significant sense of emotional vulnerability for the police officer:

"If the job becomes your life, and you don't control your job, then you don't control your life."

What *Do* Officers Control?

There clearly are dimensions of the police role that law enforcement officers have absolute autonomy and control over. Officers clearly control

- their integrity
- their professionalism
- how well they do the job assigned

However, forces outside the officers themselves control almost everything else concerning the police role. These other forces control major elements of the individual officer's cop role:

- the agency
- the administration or management
- the courts
- the constitution
- the politics of the department
- the local, state, or federal elected officials

Officers control 100 percent of their integrity and professionalism. Everything else—policies, uniforms, required procedures, budget, assignments, organizational goals, and just about every other central aspect of the officer's role—is controlled by someone else.

Officers control 100 percent of their integrity and professionalism.

Singular Identity
Controlled by Others

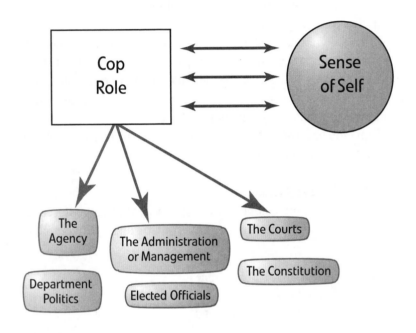

Injustices

Many police officers have firsthand experience of the dynamic of having control taken away from them by forces further up the administrative food chain. How many good cops have overidentified with their jobs and had the rude awakening of

- being taken out of detectives
- getting pulled off the SWAT team
- being transferred back to uniformed patrol
- being transferred to midnight shift
- being transferred out of K-9 and having the dog taken away
- losing a good case to another detective or agent
- having the worst car in the fleet

It is the rare officer who has not experienced this phenomenon at some point in his or her police career. In the vernacular of the average cop, this is called *getting screwed*. Sometimes the transfers are done for some rational reason that makes sense, and sometimes they are "total bullshit" and reflect some manager, boss, or administrator flexing muscle only to demonstrate that he or she has the capacity to make your life miserable.

Officers unaware of the dynamic of emotional overidentification taking place in their lives can find themselves going through significant emotional turmoil. A sense of vulnerability leads to emotional susceptibility, which is a feeling of being constantly at emotional risk. The officer who has difficulty with overidentification with the police role runs the risk of feeling constantly in danger from the forces that control the police role. This can become an ever present sense of feeling emotionally at risk, vulnerable, susceptible, threatened, and paranoid.

Emotional Effects of a Singular Identity

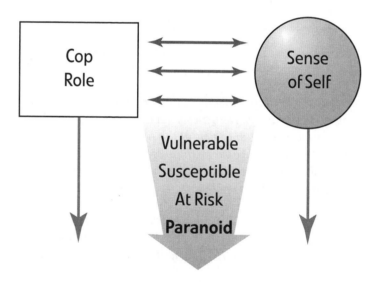

As some force outside of their control affects the cop role, officers who overidentify with the police role find the impact on their personal lives not far behind. The sense of self also takes a hit.

Here, for example, is our homicide detective when he is called into the boss's office and told he is being taken off a major homicide investigation, even though he knows he is the best detective for the case. Worse yet, he is told to go get his uniforms ready because he is being transferred out of detectives and back to patrol. The figure on page 82 demonstrates the sense of risk the officer experiences every time some force outside his or her control affects the cop role. It is at this point that our homicide detective and probably the vast majority of other well-intentioned officers who have not practiced good emotional survival skills begin feeling overwhelming senses of distrust, anger, and open hostility toward the management hierarchy of their own agencies. It is at this point that the police officers who have been unknowingly experiencing the hypervigilance rollercoaster become engaged in the psychological conflict that stems from overidentification with a role they do not control.

The Blame Game

After listening to officers, an observer might encounter the typical phenomenon that engulfs many well-intentioned but poorly informed officers. The locations of the agencies might be quite different, but the officers' responses are almost always identical:

"I can handle the assholes on the street. The assholes that I can't handle are the ones running this place."

"I can do the job if the assholes in the administration would just let us do the damn job. Hell, they don't want us doing the job. The surest way to get in trouble at this agency is to go out on the streets and do police work. The bosses will screw you to the wall if you do good cop work. They want us out there making kumbaya with all the assholes."

"Oh yeah, right, the chief is going to tell me how to make a traffic stop. Let me ask you, when the hell was the last time the chief made a traffic stop? Hell, he hasn't seen the ball since the kick-off."

"You think I'm making this shit up? Well, I'll tell you I've been at this agency for fifteen years—same circus, different clowns. I wouldn't trust these management assholes as far as I can throw them. I was talking to my lawyer yesterday and he said, 'Document it, or better yet, get it on tape,' so when we take them to court this time we'll stick it to them."

"I buy a lottery ticket every Friday and I tell you what, if I hit the lottery, I'm going to pile all my police department bullshit

*on the front lawn of my house and one of those pencil-necked
assholes in the administration can come by and pick it up."*

*"The door ain't going to hit me in the ass. I mean it, you just
watch, fifteen more years and I'm the hell out of here. I'll be
gone. I'm getting the hell out of here."*

Many officers can close their eyes and picture someone in their
agency making these statements, maybe even themselves. Unfortunately,
the orientation reflected in these statements can actually typify the second half of many law enforcement officers' careers. If you analyze each
of the statements, the common theme is a belief that a wrong has been
done to the officer by the agency, either at this time or at some time in
the past. There is the continuing belief that the agency did something
to injure the individual officer by violating some standard of ethical
treatment or fair play. Although on occasion this is clearly the case,
many times the officer's beliefs about having been victimized reflect
only a generalized and paranoid distrust of everything and everybody in
management and administrative roles. These statements, by some officers, say more about the respective officer's worldview of distrust than
they do about whatever person,
organization, or event on which they
are commenting. Many officers,
particularly those who have overidentified with the police role, can
find themselves seeing the world

> *Nobody, but nobody, will escape
> from a police career with their
> professional virginity intact.
> Everyone gets screwed by the
> agency at least one time.*

from the viewpoint of victims of some poorly defined organizational
conspiracy. They might do well to adapt some basic and overriding beliefs
concerning a police career, such as the following basic truth:

Nobody, but nobody, will escape from a police career with their
professional virginity intact. Everyone gets screwed by the agency at
least one time.

Getting screwed does not mean being disciplined when an officer
deserves to be disciplined. Getting screwed means officers receive the
discipline—the letter of reprimand or days off without pay—when they
really shouldn't have; or officers get transferred involuntarily when
they are doing a good job; or officers don't get the transfer or promo-
tion that they deserve.

They got screwed.

Life Lessons

If you disagree with this premise, or want to know how to prepare for the potential injustice of a police career, go back to your respective agency, find one of the "big bosses," assume the position, and say "Do me, Do me, Do me." Get it over with and get over it. There is life after not getting the assignment you wanted or not getting the newer patrol car you thought you deserved. You know, the one that was manufactured just for you.

One can always see officers who don't understand this dynamic and who can't let it go. They are constantly upset with the agency over the wrongdoings or unfairness to which they have been subjected. They will recite a litany of wrongful acts committed by the chief, sheriff, or special agent in charge over the past fifteen or twenty years. They appear very focused on what wrong has been done to them and how they are totally untrusting of the agency. Have you ever noticed how these individuals appear consumed by the wrongful acts of the individuals running their agency? Stop and think about this for a moment. These officers have unwittingly fallen into the most common dilemma experienced by police officers. They do not understand how they have become trapped in this endless conflict with their own agency and, more important, they don't know how to get out of it. The only coping mechanisms they believe they have at their disposal don't work:

- They bitch about it.
- They file grievances.
- They file lawsuits.
- They quit the agency.
- They file stress disability claims.
- They orchestrate votes of "no confidence" against the chief.
- They say, "I don't give a damn anymore, and I ain't doing shit for this place anymore."

Although some of these strategies do have an appropriate time and place, none of them is going to provide officers with a capacity to understand their focused, all-consuming anger and rage at the agency. It is easy to determine which law enforcement officers in any agency have fallen prey to this dynamic. Usually it is the best officers, or at least the individuals who formerly were the best officers, the men and women victimized by the hypervigilance rollercoaster, those who unwittingly put the rest of their lives on hold. They became twenty-six-hour-a-day police officers. The reality of being one-dimensional is that officers' sense of self is totally invested in a role they don't control. Ironically, those who do control the officers' role (and therefore their sense of self) are the very people the officers have the least amount of trust or faith in—the administration or management of the agency.

The more that officers focus in on only their police role and become consumed by what has happened to them because of the agency, the more the overcommitted officers empower the very individuals they least trust.

Victims are defined as people who have control taken away from them.

This can be where the previously idealistic and motivated officer begins thinking of herself or himself clearly as a victim. Victims are defined as people who have control taken away from them.

From Singular Identity to Victim

Victims Have No Control

Not only are officers thinking like victims, they are thinking like paranoid victims. They have become overinvested emotionally in the police role and have made the police role the major element in their lives. Now, after being screwed by the agency, they realize they don't control their police role and therefore they don't control the major element in their lives. Remember that possessing a sense of control over one's life, destiny, and sense of self is central to emotional well-being and psychological autonomy. To not control the major part of their lives is extremely unsettling for officers to experience.

Officers experience intense and profound emotions when going through this dynamic:

"I can't stand being around these assholes."

"One of these days I'm going to get a chance to stick it to them, you just watch."

"I busted my ass working the streets for these people, and they just don't give a shit."

"I can't tell you how much time I have given this place without claiming overtime, and now they tag me for leaving fifteen minutes early and they're talking about giving me a day off without pay."

"I get so pissed off at this place, I just don't give a damn anymore about anything."

"I document everything I do and see around here. I play CYA big time."

"These assholes piss me off so much anymore that I can't get them out of my mind."

These officers are defining themselves as victims. This doesn't mean that the grievances they profess lack merit or didn't in fact take place; what the term "victim" means in this context is that they now wear their victim status as a badge of honor. They begin in some cases to obsess over the issue. Every so often a little bitching is probably good for the soul and psyche; however, becoming trapped in the victim role can be a career-ending experience, at least ending the positive contribution to the organization that the officer had in all likelihood previously made. Remember from the officer's orientation and worldview, the situation also has significant elements of distrust. The hypervigilance she or he learned on the streets to survive is now focused on surviving the internal organization.

> *"I can handle the assholes on the street; I just can't handle the assholes in management."*

Officers *Do* Control Their Personal Lives

As discussed in chapter 4, the term "asshole" stems from the officer feeling in jeopardy or at risk from a person or location. Ironically, as the years of a police career pass, many officers feel most vulnerable and at risk when dealing with their own agencies. The reason for this feeling of vulnerability is that the agency controls the police role and, because of the long-term effect of the hypervigilance rollercoaster, the officer has long since abandoned the one realm where he or she has absolute control—the bottom half of the rollercoaster. Think about the rollercoaster shown on page 91. An officer is getting all of her or his sense of self and feelings of accomplishment from the upper phase of the rollercoaster, but who controls the upper phase? The agency controls the upper phase. Which phase does the officer control? The officer has absolute control of the lower phase of the rollercoaster, his or her personal life. But what if officers are doing nothing in the lower phase? What do they control? *They control nothing.*

Remember: Victims have no control.

Without training in emotional survival, the rollercoaster sets up officers to think, act, and live like victims, to not invest their energy, emotions, and sense of self in the phase of the rollercoaster that they do in fact control, the bottom or off-duty phase. It's a clear catch-22: Officers must maintain hypervigilance to perform and survive on the streets and practice good officer safety, yet it is this same hypervigilance that can cause officers to relinquish control of their personal lives. They cannot lower the upper phase of the rollercoaster. They *must* maintain the elevated physical state of heightened awareness of potential risk while functioning as officers. Without training and awareness of the rollercoaster, officers return home and experience the pendulum effect. The magic chair captures them. Weeks become months, and months become years across the span of a police career as the "I usta" syndrome robs officers of any other interests or outlets. The good officers, the most enthusiastic officers, put all their energy and heartfelt commitment into one thing—trying to be the best cops they can be. Ironically, it is the nonpolice support systems that, when they remain intact, determine if the officers remain good cops for the duration of the entire police career—not good cops for just a few short years of high activity followed by fifteen or more years of perceiving themselves as victims and relinquishing their commitment to be the best cops they can be.

> *"I usta bust my ass for these people, but not anymore.*
> *I discovered a long time ago, the more you do, the more they*
> *screw with you. I pulled my horns in years ago."*

If officers continue to underinvest emotionally in the phase they actually control, they only intensify their victim status. By not addressing the bottom half of the rollercoaster and by trying to obtain all emotional and social needs from the on-duty phase, the police role, at the expense of strengthening the nonpolice roles, officers are in a trap. Without some assistance, they won't be able to get out. They don't know what is taking place in their lives emotionally. They spend all emotional energy trying to right the wrong they believe is causing their problems. Victim thinking has taken over their mindset. They are preoccupied with the issue at hand, with how they have been screwed. It is the last thing they think of every night and the first thing they think of every morning. It doesn't matter what the actual issue is that has become all-consuming in the officer's life because after a few years the issues change, but the victim-based thinking doesn't change.

Remember, these officers are not only thinking like victims, they are thinking like paranoid victims. So if a friend or coworker attempts to ask these officers to "just let it go" or "move on with life," the officers will start recounting the wrongful acts perpetrated against them

The Hypervigilance Biological Rollercoaster®: Disengagement from Personal Life

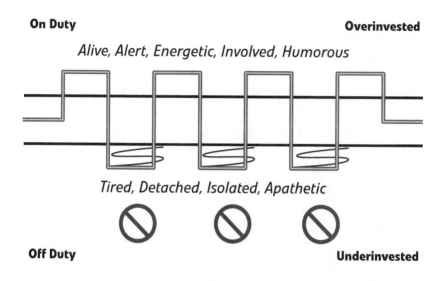

On Duty   **Overinvested**

Alive, Alert, Energetic, Involved, Humorous

Tired, Detached, Isolated, Apathetic

Off Duty   **Underinvested**

The agency controls the upper phase of the rollercoaster (the police role).
The officer controls the lower phase of the rollercoaster (the personal life role).

by the agency, and they won't accept the coworker's perspective. Further, victim officers will then feel the coworker has sold out to the agency and that they, the victim officers, are the only "true defenders of the faith." They are the only ones who have the courage to stand up and tell it like it is. They are blind to the fact that the world, as they see it, has become condensed to only one issue—their perceived victimization by the agency. This has become the officers' new worldview.

This is not in any way meant to imply that officers should become sheep and just accept unfairness or wrongful discipline.

If a grievance needs to be filed, file it.

If a lawsuit needs to be filed, file it.

Don't become consumed by it. Or, in the words of a veteran officer: "Don't let the assholes live in your head off-duty rent-free."

Case History

Sergeant James is a sixteen-year veteran of the 1,200-officer department where he serves as a SWAT supervisor. The position Sgt. James maintains is a full-time special assignment. He has been a member of the SWAT team for twelve years, six of which have been as a supervisor. Sgt. James is well respected regionally for his expertise in SWAT-type tactical operations. He also instructs at regional, and on occasion national, tactical officer training courses. Sgt. James has received departmental citations for his performance while supervising numerous extremely intense SWAT operations. These past operations included his supervision of a multiple-hostage rescue operation, including a tactical entry under fire.

Sgt. James thoroughly enjoys his position as a SWAT supervisor and receives the respect of subordinates and supervisors alike. Although Sgt. James maintains a good relationship with a majority of personnel in his department, he has had an ongoing personality conflict, since his academy years, with one fellow officer. The individual with whom Sgt. James has the conflict has recently been promoted to the rank of commander. After several transfers of other departmental command personnel have taken place, Sgt. James finds himself working directly under the supervision of the commander with whom he has the conflict. From Sgt. James's perspective, his role is one of professional expertise, and he relates that he has no problem working for anyone. He believes it is strictly a professional role and any former personality conflicts are not important. The new commander, however, does not share Sgt. James's feelings on the issue of letting bygones be bygones and decides almost immediately upon taking command of SWAT that Sgt. James needs to be displaced from his position and returned to uniformed patrol as a patrol supervisor. Sgt. James has not worked the field in a uniformed capacity for the past six years.

The commander also realizes that he cannot arbitrarily transfer Sgt. James from his position as a SWAT supervisor due to the exemplary service and performance that Sgt. James has maintained during his tenure in that assignment. The commander, realizing that he cannot directly and arbitrarily make the transfer occur, creates a new departmental policy requiring mandatory rotation of all special assignment supervisors every four years. The end result of the commander's new policy is that Sgt. James is removed from SWAT team assignments and forced back into uniformed patrol. Sgt. James, who is typically a positive supervisor with an excellent attitude, becomes increasingly cynical toward the department. He becomes increasingly verbal about his beliefs: "The department screwed me and put me back on patrol, forgetting my twelve years of SWAT experience, just because the commander had it in for me."

In reviewing the case of Sgt. James, most veteran police officers can identify, from their own experience, an almost identical case. Clearly a dedicated and competent officer has experienced a major setback, professionally and personally. Sgt. James's future will be determined not by what the commander did to him but rather by how Sgt. James personally adjusts to the change. A victim would be able to view the situation and articulate how the agency screwed Sgt. James, that this is just another example of how the agency showed itself to be thankless and unappreciative of a competent and dedicated employee's years of contribution and service. It would be hard to argue that the victim perspective was without foundation, since in fact a petty and personally vindictive commander *did* screw Sgt. James. The real question would be: Is Sgt. James willing to remain a victim and focus in on what he does not control or does he want to become a survivor and focus in on what he does control?

It's expected that Sgt. James will go through an adjustment period, holding hard feelings toward the agency, but what if the hard feelings don't subside? What if the hard feelings start becoming the way Sgt. James views every encounter he has with the agency? Depending on where the person is within the agency hierarchy when they view Sgt. James, they might draw different conclusions. A member of the management team seeing or hearing Sgt. James talk of his attitude toward the agency could form the conclusion that he is just another malcontent, some poorly performing employee who doesn't appreciate how good he has it. Someone viewing Sgt. James from the rank and file could draw the conclusion that Sgt. James is justified in how he feels toward the agency and is perfectly justified in doing as little as possible because "those unappreciative assholes in the administration screwed over another good cop."

Both perspectives are probably equally incorrect. The management perspective is not focusing in on what is taking place personally for Sgt. James and is only viewing his behavior today. The rank and file individuals are not taking into consideration that Sgt. James has an obligation to provide competent police services to his agency, regardless of whether he agrees with the position to which he is presently assigned. Sgt. James, however, is the one left holding the bag emotionally. He is the one who has the emotional reactions to what has taken place in his life. He is the one who has to emotionally balance the sense of loss of a position he highly valued. He also is the one who will have to balance the change in terms of how he views his entire police career. He can be a victim and go with that theme for the remainder of his career—many officers do. He can also be a survivor and focus on the things he does control.

Victims focus on what they do not control.

Survivors focus on what they do control.

Sgt. James has several strategies available to him, some productive and some self-defeating. He could attempt to rationalize his lack of commitment and dedication to being back in patrol as a response to the manner in which he has been treated by the agency. He could justify his minimal performance in his new position by stating, "If they don't care, why should I?" He could start a new career orientation of coasting and doing as little as possible or even become actively involved in attempting to undermine the agency administration and management.

These strategies are based on victim-based thinking. They involve considering the actions of individuals outside himself as the determining and responsible cause of his actions. They involve focusing in on what he does *not* control—the actions of others. For some people, who have been living their entire lives as self-perceived victims, this seems perfectly natural and rational.

"It is the commander's fault that Sgt. James has turned into a malcontent. If they hadn't transferred him, this never would have happened."

This seems perfectly logical to the victim-based thinker. It means that other people determine Sgt. James's thinking and professional dedication; it is not Sgt. James's responsibility to control his own level of dedication and motivation. *If they hadn't transferred him out, this never would have happened.* This is probably true, at least in part, but when would it have happened? The commander certainly is responsible for being a petty, vindictive, self-serving individual who abuses his professional authority to punish hard-working and dedicated police officers. He is without a doubt a very poor manager and an even poorer example of a leader. Sgt. James, however, is responsible for his response to the transfer. A survivor orientation is necessary to adjust to this challenging situation. Waiting for the world, and particularly the world of a police officer, to change and be asshole-free is going to be a very long wait.

Good Cops Can Be as Overinvested as Malcontent Cops

Learning a survivor orientation is quite difficult, particularly if the officer has not been trained in the concepts of emotional overinvestment and has never heard of the hypervigilance rollercoaster. The first victims of the rollercoaster are the hard-working and dedicated police officers and their families. The second "victim" is the career itself. Officers who assume the victim orientation begin rationalizing and justifying to themselves behavior that they previously would have found unacceptable. Many people might encourage Sgt. James to back off caring at work. They might encourage him not to give a damn, but think about the actual effect that such behavior would have on Sgt. James

> *Officers who assume the victim orientation begin rationalizing and justifying to themselves behavior that they previously would have found unacceptable.*

and countless other good police officers in similar situations. It would mean they are rejecting their own internal core values of service and dedication. They would begin defining themselves as the opposite of what they previously stood for. They would begin defining themselves in oppositional or antagonistic terms to their previously held sense of self. Instead of being the twenty-six-hour-a-day police officers who love their role, they would become the twenty-six-hour-a-day officers who hate the job. Both are examples of significant overinvestment emotionally in a job or dimension of their lives they do not control. The only difference between the two orientations is that one maintains a positive charge emotionally and the other a negative charge.

Malcontent officers are defining their lives by the job role as much as positive, pro-agency, enthusiastic officers are. Malcontents define themselves by taking the opposite orientation or position to how the job is defined by the organization. Whether positive or negative over-investment, the officers are allowing their sense of self to be defined by individuals other than themselves. In both cases, this orientation enables victim-based thinking to thrive. Malcontent officers also have a somewhat self-destructive orientation because they now reject the very core values of commitment and enthusiasm that previously were central to their own self definition. That our best officers are most affected illustrates why teaching officers how to become emotional survivors needs to be a high priority in law-enforcement training; unfortunately, it is rarely, if ever, a subject of importance to either organizations or the individual officer.

Victim-Based Thinking

What happens if the victim orientation becomes the predominant way of viewing the world for Sgt. James and countless other law enforcement officers who, from their perspective, have been screwed by the agency? What if they begin seeing all events in their lives as affected or colored by the treatment they received from the organization? What happens if all decisions these officers are required to make are potentially contaminated by a "victim tint"? Do police officers potentially compromise their professionalism and integrity when they define themselves as victims?

If you ask people the question, "What do victims want?" you will hear a variety of answers:

- restitution
- fairness
- righting the wrong done to them
- retribution

All of these terms are basically a more socially acceptable way of expressing our desire for revenge or payback. What each of these desires involves is a manner of taking back control that has been taken away by the offending party. In the criminal justice system, each of these concepts is particularly important when a genuine victim has been violated. This is the reason *real* victims have a chance to speak at criminal-sentencing hearings, or the reason juries award damages to real victims in civil court claims.

What about the *self-perceived* victim in the workplace who wants to recover or take back an intangible, such as enthusiasm or dedication? This is particularly difficult because what these people want to recover—motivation, enthusiasm, and idealism about the job—are in reality in their control to begin with. It is not the person transferring Sgt. James who controls the sergeant's motivation and idealism. Sgt. James controls that. The commander only controls the assignment; Sgt. James controls his emotional reaction to the assignment.

Some individuals in law enforcement, once they become self-perceived victims, can cease investing in the work role many years before they retire or leave. Once officers see themselves as having been victimized, it can be hard to let it go and return to enthusiastic and committed work, particularly if the offending commander is still present in the organization. Without assistance or insight into the dynamics of malcontentism and overinvestment, these officers potentially begin a predictable system of thinking that can start guiding their judgment and behavior. When officers begin seeing themselves as victims, they begin possessing many of the clearly identifiable attributes listed in the box below.

Victim Attributes

- merging of personal and professional roles
- hypersensitivity to change (all change is a personal assault)
- rigidity and inflexibility
- ever present feeling of threat from the organization
- belief one is being controlled or persecuted by the agency
- need to retaliate against management hierarchy for perceived wrongs
- social isolation from others in the organization except a few "true believers"
- grandiose sense of self importance: "I'm one of the best cops in this department."
- exaggerated perception of past accomplishments
- internalized sense of entitlement

Unfortunately, the above list of attributes paints a picture of a person who has lost the way. Many good police officers possess many of the above traits. They may also report a generalized feeling of being caught in a world where they cannot escape—the ever present emotions these attributes create.

Entitlement

Of the traits listed above, one of the most damaging to law enforcement officers and agencies alike is the internalized sense of entitlement. A belief in entitlement can begin driving an officer's decision making. This belief can be explained as an occupationally acquired worldview that because of everything police officers have to put up with, all the B.S., they deserve a break. The foundation of entitlement orientation is in victim-based thinking. Entitlement can permit the officers and agencies to rationalize behavior they would not normally engage in and see it as perfectly acceptable. Victim-based thinking also lets the officers blame others or externalize responsibility for their own behavior. To illustrate this point, you might ask a group of officers the following question:

"How many of you think it is acceptable to go out in the parking garage, select a car someone personally owns, take your car key out, and put a key scratch or gouge down the entire length of the car?"

The obvious response from the officers will be that the behavior is unacceptable. It is not appropriate to vandalize someone's car. When you ask why this isn't all right to do, you'll receive several answers:

- "It is morally wrong."
- "It is unlawful."
- "I wasn't raised that way."
- "I don't do stuff like that."
- "We arrest people who do stuff like that."
- "You could get cited or arrested."
- "You could get fired."
- "I wouldn't want anyone to do that to me."

Each officer sees that damaging another person's property is unacceptable, inappropriate, and clearly criminal behavior. However, if you present a slightly different scenario, the answers can change:

"You go out in the parking garage and you find a large scratch or key gouge in your personal car, and you ask, "Who did this?" and several of your friends come forward and identify the person who damaged your car. Would it be easier now to go put a key scratch or gouge in the car belonging to the person who scratched your car?"

Some folks may say, "Two wrongs don't make a right," but the majority of responses will be along the following lines:

"I'd scratch his car right after I kicked his butt."

In one situation, the response to scratch the car is wrong, but when a perception of having been victimized is injected, the response changes. The experience or perception of having been victimized changes the rules for many individuals:

An eye for an eye
A tooth for a tooth
A paint job for a paint job

Because many law enforcement officers have not received even basic training in the area of emotional survival, they develop the world-view of having been victimized. The hypervigilance rollercoaster and "I usta" syndrome have taken their toll and the officer can begin living life as an emotionally overinvested, self-perceived victim.

Situational versus Core Values

What can happen to officers whose worldview is tainted by this belief of having been victimized? How does it affect the officers who each day are still required to perform their professional duties under emotionally demanding and, at times, physically threatening situations? How does the lack of an emotional survival orientation and skill-set affect officers who must face the daily requirement of making a full range of decisions that can demand the wisdom of Solomon?

The decisions law enforcement officers are required to make demand individuals who are emotionally balanced and are not perceptually tainted by a victim orientation. Permitting law enforcement officers to make decisions from a victim perspective without benefit of emotional survival awareness is grossly unfair to law enforcement officers themselves, as well as the public they serve. The victim orientation robs the officer of the benefit of using a lifetime of internalized core values as the foundation for decision making. The *core values* become *situational values*.

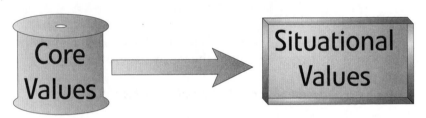

The movement from core values to situational values, based on a belief of having been victimized, permits officers to rationalize behavior they previously would not have accepted in themselves. It also permits the officers to project blame for their own behavior onto other persons.

"If that guy didn't want his car scratched, he shouldn't have scratched mine."

"If they wanted Sgt. James to remain a dedicated officer, they should have left him in SWAT and not screwed with him."

At first glance, these statements seem logical enough because there is a factual basis for having been wronged and violated. On further examination, however, these statements are just another example of the contaminated thinking police officers hear each day on the street:

- "He called me a name. That's why I shot him."
- "He cut me off in traffic. That's why I ran into the back of his car."
- "She was messing around with my man. That's why I stabbed her."
- "He was talking trash to me. That's why I kicked his ass."
- "She owed me ten dollars. That's why I messed up her car."
- "They were playing the music real loud. That's why I threw the rock at their window."
- "He was on our turf. That's why we wasted him."

And on and on and on and on *ad nauseam*. Basically, these people are saying, "It's the other person's fault how I behaved. After all, I can't be expected to be a responsible person who is held accountable for my own behavior. I'm entitled to do what I did."

The basic paradigm of victim-based entitlement thinking:

> *"They screwed with me, which is why I engaged in this behavior."*

> *"The rules don't apply to me because of what I had to put up with."*

You would think police officers would be highly sensitive to the reasoning of people who abdicate responsibility for their own behavior using pathological excuse mongering. Every day officers have to listen to the dregs of society using self-perceived-victim rationalizations as an excuse not to be held accountable for a wide spectrum of outrageous, even criminal, behavior. Possibly the daily exposure of police officers to individuals who refuse to accept responsibility for their own actions provides victim-based-thinking officers a paradigm for rationalizing inappropriate behavior. They can then utilize this paradigm to justifying their own professional misdeeds as officers.

> *"The chief did_____. That's why I did_____."*

> *"I got screwed by this department when they_____.*
> *That's why I did_____."*

The thinking is clearly victim-based because it projects accountability onto something the officer doesn't control—the behavior of the perceived offender. The tragedy in not addressing this type of thinking through emotional survival training and intervention is that it can ruin the careers and lives of many good police officers. By not providing training in emotional survival so that police officers can clearly see the difference between self-perceived victims and emotional survivors, law enforcement organizations don't give officers the ability to maintain their most valued asset: their core values. This failure of adequate career preparation allows officers to justify their behavior against a standard of situational values. It basically sets up the officers for failure and devastation in their personal *and* professional lives. When victim-based thinking and entitlement take over officers' worldviews, they can progress down a predictable path of inappropriate behavior patterns.

Acts of Omission

Good officers do not show their victim status by going out and doing something wrong. They go out and stop doing something right. Officers initially show they are self-perceived victims by lowering their levels of production, their standard for professional duties. Self-initiated activities, such as traffic citations, reduce. Officers justify the nonperformance of job duties based on their self-perception of having been victimized by the agency. They begin engaging in acts of omission.

> *Good officers do not show their victim status by going out and doing something wrong. They go out and stop doing something right.*

"If they don't care, why should I?"

"You never get in trouble for the stop you don't make."

"I answer my calls. That's all I get paid to do!"

At first, it might seem like acts of omission of professional duties are not a major worry for the officer but rather a production problem for the agency. But these acts are very much a problem for both officer *and* agency. When the officer can rationalize any wrongdoing, whether by omission of duties or by active engagement in wrongdoing, the officer is violating his or her own core values and beginning a journey down a path that can have both personal and professional ramifications. Enthusiasm is replaced by diffuse anger. The active go-getter officer of a few years ago can become the officer who sees nothing and hears nothing and does nothing. Officers justify and rationalize all of this behavior because of the violation done to them by the agency years ago. Some entire law enforcement agencies operate as a subculture of victim-based entitlement thinkers, which provides significant peer support for the nonperformance of duties. Acts of omission can be demonstrated by the following case example.

Case History

Officer Kerri Smith is a nine-year veteran officer of a medium-size sheriff's department. Her entire career to date has been in uniformed street patrol. The agency at which she works also maintains a large county jail and requires all officers to rotate to the jail for two-year tours-of-duty during their careers. Officer Smith has just received her notice of being rotated to perform her jail tour on the next scheduled shift change in ninety days. (Her agency gives the ninety-day rotation notice to permit officers ample time to arrange personal issues, such as child care, because the jail uses a different shift-rotation format then the patrol division uses.) Officer Smith, who is an active street officer, thinks placing experienced officers in a detention capacity is both a poor management strategy and a waste of good police officers' street experience. She approaches the chief and attempts to argue against her having to do the mandatory jail rotation, telling the chief "the department should hire animal control officers to work with the assholes in the jail and leave the good officers on the street, so they can keep the jail full by doing good police work." The chief informs Officer Smith that he doesn't particularly care if Smith thinks the policy is appropriate or fair and tells her "'Fair' is what you pay to ride on the bus." The chief clearly informs Officer Smith she can expect to be rotated to the jail in ninety days as planned.

Officer Smith, realizing she will rotate to the jail in ninety days no matter what she says or does, ceases doing any self-initiated street police work during the time her rotation is pending. She regularly sees traffic violations occur in her presence and takes no enforcement action. On calls for service to which she is dispatched, she rarely makes an arrest and her officer reports are little more then one- or two-line summaries of what has taken place. She only minimally conducts investigations and generally has ceased working as a police officer. Her supervisor on several occasions has called her on the radio and Officer Smith has failed to respond, telling the supervisor she didn't hear the radio transmission, when in fact she did hear the transmission and just refused to answer. She tells her fellow officers:

"Screw the department. If they want me to be a jailer for two years, why should I act like a street cop?"

Officer Smith certainly sees herself as having been victimized by the agency at which she has worked for nine years. She certainly can gain professional agreement from many law enforcement professionals about her negative thoughts on using experienced street officers in the jail. She would probably gain agreement that the chief was harsh and insensitive in speaking to an experienced officer in the manner he spoke to Officer Smith. She could also obtain agreement that the chief was following a foolish personnel strategy in the jail-rotation policy. Although the chief is clearly responsible for poor leadership and possibly poor personnel practices, who in reality is responsible for Officer Smith's lack of performance of her police duties on the street during the ninety days prior to her jail rotation?

If Officer Smith is waiting for a time in her career when she will be free of foolish departmental policies, she might have a long wait. It is quite understandable that she would be highly disappointed in her transfer to the jail. It is also quite understandable that she feels the transfer policy is an example of poor police personnel management, but how does she get past the reality of the transfer? Although she is not able to change the transfer itself, is Officer Smith helpless to overcome the emotional reaction to her situation? Are the acts of omission that Officer Smith is engaging in destructive only to the overall productivity of the agency? How are her actions and change of heart affecting Officer Smith herself? What are the effects on Officer Smith herself of daily violating her own core values of dedicated service and professional enthusiasm? Does engaging in a work orientation that is directly opposite to how she has worked for the past nine years affect Officer Smith personally?

By violating her own core values, because she believes she has been victimized, Officer Smith is actually doing harm to herself and her own sense of self-esteem. Although it is easy to blame the agency, the chief, or a personnel rotation policy, Officer Smith is acting like a self-perceived victim and is actually beginning to self-destruct. She sees herself daily permit traffic violators to avoid citations. She is actually invalidating, in her own eyes, the importance and significance of the past nine years of admirable police service that has typified her career. Her victim-based assessment of what has happened to her permits her to say events outside of her control are causing the change in her professional orientation.

She can begin seeing herself not as a free-standing professional law enforcement officer, but as merely a puppet whose professional demeanor is controlled by others. Clearly others control the assignment, but who controls Officer Smith's professional demeanor? She thinks everything is out of her control:

"I am not responsible for my own demeanor, values, enthusiasm, and integrity. Someone else controls that."

The irony and paradox of this type of thinking is that it actually empowers, in the officer's mind, the very individuals who have caused the professional setback. If Officer Smith acknowledges her extreme disappointment in the transfer to the jail and respectfully expresses her belief that the jail transfer policy is inappropriate and archaic, yet continues to be a productive street police officer, several things will likely happen. She will still do her two years in the jail whether she likes it or not, yet she will be able to retain her orientation that she controls her sense of self and professional demeanor. She will be focusing on what she values and what she controls, which is being an effective and dedicated police officer.

Some officers could confuse the issue of what Officer Smith really controls and say, "She was demonstrating what she controlled by not being productive. She controls her self-initiated activity level." Although she does control her self-initiated activity level, by engaging in acts of omission, she is violating her own core values and damaging her sense of self-esteem as an officer and a person. Officer Smith is also violating an oath of office she took as a police officer.

Officer Smith's acts of omission only reinforce and further her worldview of herself as a victim, not as a survivor. A survivor might say:

"I hate the thought of working in the jail for two years. I think it is a totally inappropriate policy, and the department should hire animal control officers to deal with the assholes in the jail, but I have always done as good a job as I can as an officer, and I will do as good a job as I can in there and count my days until I can get back on the street."

This is not just a strategy of being a good employee; it is a strategy to focus in on your core values and realize you, not the agency or organizational administration, are in control of your own behavior and demeanor. This survival strategy would permit Officer Smith to dislike the assignment but keep her core values and orientation as a survivor intact. Victims unfortunately begin acting like victims in all phases of their lives, and something such as a transfer can precipitate into a series of cascading actions that ruin lives and careers as, unfortunately, happened with Officer Smith.

Case History *(continued)*

As Officer Smith's case unfolds, she begins developing her victim orientation aggressively during the ninety days prior to her rotation. She announces that almost everything that has comes out of the "head shed," or administration, is "bullshit." Her productivity is down, and she is no longer the enthusiastic officer she had been throughout her nine-year career. She dreads the thought of going into the jail for several reasons. She detests the nature of the work involved in being a jail officer, but she realizes she will also miss the camaraderie and social networking that has been part of her work experience up to this point. Her only friends are her coworkers on the street.

Officer Smith is also a typical officer who has never given any significant thought to her own emotional survival strategies. She has never understood its importance and has received no training in the concepts of the hypervigilance rollercoaster or being emotionally overinvested in the job at the expense of other support systems. She begins her jail rotation resentful, angry, and uncooperative with her new supervisors and coworkers. She particularly dislikes those officers who have volunteered to remain in the jail bureau after their mandatory two-year rotation, calling them "lifers" and "losers." She finds the duties of being a jail officer "little more than babysitting assholes." As the months inside the jail pass, Officer Smith finds herself increasingly moody in her personal life. She works her shift at the jail and returns to her home, watches television, and generally is captured by the magic chair. Every day becomes a cycle of work and a sedentary off-duty lifestyle.

Approximately six months after beginning her rotation into the jail (or "zoo," as Officer Smith calls it) she is assigned to work as a booking officer, handling incoming prisoners. This position can be particularly provocative and confrontational in the jail because it is the point where arresting officers process inmates and transfer custody to the jail division. It is the scene of numerous physical confrontations.

Shortly after starting this new position, Officer Smith is taking custody of an inmate from three arresting street officers, all of whom have already completed their two-year mandatory jail rotation, when they begin ribbing Officer Smith about doing her "turn in the barrel" (her jail rotation). When Officer Smith states, "My tour as a babysitter for assholes is 25 percent over," the arrestee, not appreciating the comment about "assholes," tells Officer Smith that the "only assholes around this place are the ones with badges." Officer Smith, in the presence of the other officers, punches the prisoner and slams the prisoner's head against the wall, telling her to "shut her mouth or she'll shut it for her." The prisoner complies with Officer Smith's demand, but through her public defender files an internal affairs complaint and a civil lawsuit against Officer Smith for brutality.

The booking desk of the jail, due to its provocative and confrontational location, is one of the departmental locations where all officer-inmate interactions are videotaped by an openly displayed surveillance camera. The videotape clearly shows Officer Smith striking the handcuffed prisoner without any signs of physical threat from the prisoner that would warrant such physical actions in defense by Officer Smith. Officer Smith is terminated from employment for her actions and is charged with assault and civil rights violation by the prosecutor's office. Officer Smith, being charged with a criminal act, is required to financially fund her own legal defense and, due to the videotaped evidence against her, she is forced to accept a plea agreement for assault. Although she is not required by her plea agreement to do jail time, she is convicted of a crime and is decertified by her state P.O.S.T. as a peace officer, thus ending a law enforcement career and losing a retirement package that she was only eleven years from earning. She ultimately loses her home due to loss of income. If you ask Officer Smith how all this happened in a matter of a few months, she will gladly tell you:

"It was the fault of the chief and his damned jail-rotation policy."

"It was the fault of the assholes in the jail."

"It was the fault of the damned Big Brother snitch cameras."

Acts of Commission

Officer Smith's story points out the tragedies that can befall good officers once they become obsessed with a victim-based thinking orientation. Acts of *omission* yield to acts of *commission*. The continuum passes from passive avoidance of duties due to the belief of having been victimized to the active commission of rule violations. First, the officer breaks or ignores administrative rules; ultimately, criminal violations can occur. Officer Smith was a good cop. She just didn't have a clue about emotional survival nor her developing victim orientation. Her anger kept feeding on itself until she began acting in ways that had not typified her behavior previously. Officer Smith did not have a record or reputation of being heavy-handed or physically aggressive while working for nine years on the street.

Here again victim-based thinkers would point to the jail-rotation policy and say it was to blame, that Officer Smith was not responsible for her behavior.

"They shouldn't put good cops into that hell hole."

They would blame the organization, after the fact, but would not have provided Officer Smith any upfront strategies to survive the jail rotation and preserve her career. Wouldn't it have been far better if Officer Smith had a strategy of emotional survival that would have permitted her to overcome the two-year rotation in the jail and see it as little more then a very bad *temporary* assignment instead of a life-changing and career-ending event?

The nine years of good police work and the hypervigilance rollercoaster set up Officer Smith to be underinvested in activities away from work. Her role of "street police officer" was foremost in her world—the rollercoaster had taken another victim. To add insult to injury, Officer Smith also had to realize that her friends, who were the arresting officers of the prisoner she assaulted, also received significant disciplinary action partly due to Officer Smith's behavior. The videotape clearly showed that the arresting officers witnessed the assault and failed to restrain Officer Smith and also failed to report the incident to their supervisors. In this case, victim thinking made decisions along the lines of "loyalty versus integrity," a difficult choice for officers to make. Loyalty and integrity are the two cornerstones of effective and ethical law enforcement. The victim, however, forgets loyalty *and* integrity and begins viewing the world as loyalty versus integrity. As an individual's sense of self begins to get battered, the need for group and peer acceptance and approval increases. Tragically, many victim officers value loyalty to fellow officers far more than integrity and honesty.

What could Officer Smith have done when she found out she was no longer going to be working in uniformed patrol, but assigned to the jail for twenty-four months? What can Sgt. James do now that he is out of SWAT and back in uniformed patrol? It is interesting to see that one officer was a victim because he was being sent back to uniformed patrol and one officer was a victim because she was being taken out of uniformed patrol. Two good officers with lots of

> *Loyalty and integrity are the two cornerstones of effective and ethical law enforcement. The victim, however, forgets loyalty and integrity and begins viewing the world as loyalty versus integrity.*

street survival skills but no *emotional* survival skills, both facing a career-defining decision. Could the outcome have been different in Officer Smith's case? Could she have been trained to be an emotional survivor and still be on the job, waiting until she had "done her time in the barrel" to get back on the street as an officer? Back to her career and constructive service to her community, herself, and her family? The answer is clearly yes, but how could she have done it? How could these officers have become emotional survivors?

How to Become an Emotional Survivor

8

What are the attributes of emotional survivors? In all of the case histories in previous chapters, the officers appear to have one thing in common: The orientation of dedication that started and typified the beginning of their law enforcement careers and that somehow, across the course of time, became derailed. All of the officers started out idealistic, committed, and enthusiastic as they began the journey across the law enforcement years, but they all found themselves becoming embittered, angry, and disillusioned. Officer Smith's termination after being transferred to the jail division demonstrates an officer suffering significant emotional and economic loss due to a worldview that she learned, internalized, and was rewarded for as a police officer. All of the officers, ironically, had in common the orientation and worldview that their police career was central to their lives and, unfortunately, this same career became a pivotal point of loss for each of them.

Could these officers have retained across the span of a police career the idealism, enthusiasm, and motivation that typified their earlier years? If the officers understood emotional survival even remotely as well as they understood tactical or street survival, they would have in all likelihood not fallen prey to the overwhelming orientation of victim-based thinking. As survivors, they would have focused on the events that they personally could control. The officers would clearly know the difference between things that they do not control and things that they do control. This would not be a superficial Pollyanna outlook on life. It would not be a "don't worry, be happy" worldview. It would take work and dedication to be the best law enforcement officer that each of them had the potential of being and then be able each day to turn it off. Of course, it is much easier said than done to truly *leave* police work each day due to the overwhelming impact of hypervigilance and the biological rollercoaster.

A much more helpful approach for the officer leaving work is to have the goal of not so much turning off police work as *turning on* something different. The case histories in this book can typify what happens to many good law enforcement officers—everything in life becomes an "I usta." One way not to go down that road is for officers early in their careers to be trained in what it takes to maintain a sense of control in their personal lives. Training would need to take place not just with the officers but also with the officers' family members. At the beginning stages of an officer's career, this could be a parent; later on, a significant other or spouse and even children could be incorporated in the training.

A much more helpful approach for the officer leaving work is to have the goal of not so much turning off police work as **turning on** *something different.*

Survivors Practice Aggressive Personal Time Management and Goal Setting

How do you teach officers to be emotional survivors? The first step clearly is to teach officers to maintain control of their personal lives. Taking and maintaining control of one's personal life sounds like such a basic concept that it should go without saying. In reality, however, one of the first dimensions of control law enforcement officers lose is the day-to-day sense of being in charge of a schedule, of being able to control personal time. The ability to control activities, priorities, and schedules seems to disappear from officers' day-to-day experience quite soon after they become members of the law enforcement agency. The everyday real-time demands of the profession, plus the biological rollercoaster, push personal time to the back burner; it becomes of secondary importance. Such things as changing work shifts, training schedules, forced overtime, and court subpoenas take away so much of a law enforcement officer's day-to-day life. It's very easy for an officer to start developing the victim orientation.

> ### Victim Orientation
> ### (Does Not Control)
> "I have no control over my on-duty time. The job pretty much dictates what my days off and work schedules are going to be" combines with "I have no control over my off-duty personal time; the job has just taken over."
>
> ### Survivor Orientation
> ### (Does Control)
> "I need to be in charge of my daily scheduling of personal time to every extent possible."

Survivors, unlike victims, have a clear sense of personal time control. Survivors develop and continually use a specific and practical technique of personal time management, a strategy that permits them to harness the available time in their personal lives to accomplish whatever goals they choose to pursue. The development and use of a specific personal-time-management technique is extremely important for police officers for two strong reasons.

1. Police Work Isn't 24/7

Police work, by its very nature, is terribly intrusive into an individual's personal life. It's not an 8-to-5, Monday-through-Friday experience. Police agencies are 24/7, and without specific training in the subject of emotional survival, many young officers, caught up in the enthusiasm and excitement of the early career years, begin living their own lives as if their individual police role were also 24/7. The early career years of many young officers prove that the job requires working many hours beyond the typical forty-hour work week, and many profess, "There is nothing I can do about it." The victim mindset begins: "Time is out of my control." This is also fertile ground for the belief that "a personal life is an unnecessary luxury."

> *"Why do I need a personal life? I love being a cop, and going on duty seems more like fun than work."*
>
> —a three-year cop

It will not be many years before that orientation and belief changes. Teaching officers from the absolute beginning of their careers to be aggressive personal time managers is essential.

2. Police Work Destroys Spontaneity

The second major reason to train law enforcement officers in aggressive time control, or proactivity in their view of their personal time, is that they lose any sense of spontaneity in personal activities because of the biological rollercoaster. The rollercoaster robs law enforcement personnel of all spontaneity and enthusiasm after the work day has ended.

Coming home from work each day and riding the magic chair leaves officers with a view of personal time that is less than self-directed. Officers can spend the very limited hours of their personal lives sitting in front of the television set, letting life pass them by. In many ways, the officer at home, sitting in the magic chair, is acting basically like a passive victim of whatever information, entertainment, or total nonsense the television world is sending forth. This time spent in the magic chair is the beginning of a passive orientation toward personal time management. It doesn't take planning, it doesn't take goal setting, it doesn't take grabbing control of personal time. Actually it doesn't take anything. It's the basic no brainer—just click the remote control and check out. The officer begins having a reactive orientation toward the world.

Officers can spend the very limited hours of their personal lives sitting in front of the television set, letting life pass them by.

Proactive versus Reactive

It's not hard to understand how law enforcement officers lose their sense of being in charge of their personal time. First because of the physiology of hypervigilance, then because of the rather demanding and controlling interference in their personal lives by the work schedule, law enforcement officers from their earliest years on the force learn to surrender any sense of proactivity. Police work requires an on-duty *reactive* orientation as opposed to a *proactive* orientation. This reactive orientation is best understood in thinking about what many law enforcement officers do each day at work, particularly during the early stages of their careers. The uniformed police officer in a patrol capacity basically drives around the streets of his or her jurisdiction and waits for something to happen. Although community policing has a goal of having officers become more proactive in their orientation toward the police role, it will never reduce the innate reactivity of police work. Citizens will always have a need to dial 911 and have public safety professionals arrive to serve and protect them. Law enforcement officers learn early on in their career that so much of police work is having a worldview of intense observation and being ready to react.

This reactive orientation is effective for being prepared to respond when events unfold in the professional life of the law enforcement officer. A reactive orientation is tragically inadequate, however, when it becomes the officer's worldview in his or her personal life. It's a very different state of affairs to operate a patrol car as a police officer and wait for an event to take place or a call to be dispatched than it is to plan an activity with family or schedule time for physical fitness or recreation. On-duty officers learn to see the world from the reactive perspective as a means of increasing survival through hypervigilance and increased officer safety. Then they return home and attempt to continue being reactive, but there is typically nothing intense to react to, hence the feeling of let-down. So, unfortunately, some officers reactively ride the magic chair into a land of "I ustas."

A reactive orientation, which is essential for street survival, can be lethal to a personal relationship. Officers need to appreciate the requirement of reactivity on duty, but balance this with proactivity off duty. It is extremely difficult to make the transition from reactivity to proactivity due to the emotional and physical let-down of hypervigilance. What do they feel like doing after work? Nothing! What will they probably do after work? Nothing!

Officers can determine if they are falling into the reactive mode at home by reviewing their decision-making strategies to see if they are using a reactive time orientation in their personal lives. Obviously, the reactive orientation that's appropriate in their professional lives does have shortcomings when used in their personal lives.

Are You a Reactive Decision Maker?

Imagine it is your Friday evening. The workday has ended, and you've just walked in the door from work and are beginning your weekend. Does the following conversation sound familiar? If so, you are a reactive decision maker.

Officer: I don't feel like cooking, do you?

Significant other: No. I don't feel like cooking either.

Officer: Do you feel like going out to get a bite to eat?

Significant other: Sure. That sounds good. Where do you want to go?

Officer: Oh, I don't know. Any place is okay with me.

Significant other: Well, what do you feel like eating? Would you like Mexican food, Italian food, seafood? What sounds good?

Officer: Oh, I don't know. I don't care. Anything you want is okay with me. It's your call.

Significant other: Well, I don't know. Help me out. What would you like?

Officer: Look, I don't know. I've been making decisions all week. Anything's fine with me.

Significant other: Well, where do you want to go?

Officer: Where do you want to go?

Significant other: Where do you want to go?

Officer: Where do you want to go?

Significant other: Where do you want to go?

Officer: Where do you want to go?

Significant other: Where do you want to go?

Does the above dialogue exchange sound familiar? This is a perfect example of a law enforcement officer transitioning from work life, where she or he frequently handles major issues using a reactive orientation, to her or his personal life, where the proactive demands required in making a decision to go to dinner can be an overwhelming task. It sounds like the paper or plastic dilemma in chapter 6. As difficult as it is to believe, "Surprise me" and "I don't know, whatever you want is okay with me" are not signs of active engagement in conversation. This again is classic decision making (or lack thereof) at the bottom of the rollercoaster.

Victims who do not have an aggressive sense of time management would just wait and see what happens—they would "go with the flow." Survivors, on the other hand, would clearly understand that they need to develop a sense of control of their personal time. They would have been trained to develop the insight that when they return home from a shift of effective law enforcement and hypervigilance, the last thing they will want to do is make a decision. With emotional survival training, police officers learn to appreciate the important need to take control of their personal lives and become proactive. They are trained to recognize the feeling of being drained after work as a symptom of hypervigilance. More important, they are trained in how to overcome the feeling and not let it control their personal lives.

Schedule the Time

When I've interviewed police officers who have an orientation toward emotional survival, one of the fundamental characteristics these officers possess is a clearly controlled sense of personal time management. Survivors realize that the last thing they want to do when they return home is make a decision, so they develop a strategy to make the decision at an earlier point in time. How do they develop this orientation? They have been trained in the basic skills of personal time management.

> *Survivors realize that the last thing they want to do when they return home is make a decision, so they develop a strategy to make the decision at an earlier point in time.*

Ironically, victims might even know the skills and apply them in their professional lives but rarely in their personal lives. Survivors learn to be disciplined in their personal time orientation. This basically means they maintain a preplanned, written personal calendar or agenda that lists goals, requirements, and choices in their personal time that they will implement. By controlling personal time, the officer is taking control, a basic survivor orientation.

Although it sounds quite simplistic, a personal schedule is highly effective. The victim's orientation toward time is quite different from the survivor's. One law enforcement officer, a fifteen-year officer with a significant victim orientation, whom I interviewed about how he controls his personal time, gave a rather telling response:

> *"My personal life is not my responsibility.*
> *I just show up and it happens."*

Survivors would respond quite differently. They would realize the hardest step on any journey is the first. They would realize, because of emotional survival training, that upon returning home, the last thing they would like to do is make a decision about what the evening's or day's activities will be. They wouldn't leave those decisions until the last minute, when they are realistically unlikely to make them. The concept of a preplanned, personal written calendar means that officers and families have become disciplined in terms of aggressively managing their personal time. They would take the time to put into writing activities they need or want to conduct over the course of the next week or two. They would begin developing an orientation of looking forward to specific things at specific times.

The victim officer looks forward to taking his or her children camping "when things slow down at work" or "when it isn't so crazy" or "when I get a little more time on the job." The survivor officer looks forward to taking his or her children camping two weekends from now. Which officer do you think actually takes the children camping, the vague victim or the specific survivor?

These activities can be as mundane as cutting the grass or as necessary as taking the children to a dental appointment. Survivors control what is taking place in their personal lives and realize they are not controlling most of the events taking place at the police agency. By controlling their personal time, they turn off police work and turn on a personal life. This increase in off-duty activities can also create the time and opportunity to continue doing many of the activities that could have become "I ustas." Survivor officers do not disengage from family activities and responsibilities.

Make the Time

One of the major difficulties in time orientation for police officers is that many officers think they can't find the time to do what they want to do in their personal lives. They need to *make the time* to do what they want to do. Without emotional survival training, and with the development of a victim mindset, officers will find that the realities of police work and the magic chair will combine with the reactive professional orientation to fill each and every day between vigilance at work with the magic chair at home.

A Personal Time Management Calendar

Below is an example of a preplanned, written personal calendar. This calendar is a simple tool of time management that you and your family can use. Many police officers and families put their calendar on the refrigerator where it becomes a central focal point for activities and decisions that affect them.

Weekly Calendar

S	M	T	W	Th	F	Sa

If a police officer and family have developed the orientation of proactive time control, making the decision to go out to dinner might look entirely different than it does on page 116. Instead of the "wait until Friday night" strategy, the police couple might have discussed the decision several days earlier and placed it on their calendar. The couple's conversation might look different.

Officer: *What do you think if this Friday we go out to grab a bite to eat after work, just to celebrate the weekend?*

Significant other: *That sounds pretty good. Where do you want to go?*

Officer: *Let's go on down and grab a steak at that new restaurant.*

Significant other: *Sounds good. I'll give Joe and Jill a call and see if they want to join us.*

The couple then sticks it on their calendar and has something to look forward to that *they control.* If you ask officers about this interaction, "What has the officer just taken when committing, in writing, to activities in his or her personal life?" many officers will respond, "The officer has taken control." However, many of the more cynical officers, when asked what the officer has taken, will respond:

"A major step toward disappointment."

"I don't make plans. Every time you plan something, they'll screw you out of it."

"That's just total bullshit. Soon as you make plans to do something, you know one of those asshole commanders is going to have you work overtime or you'll get called out. It's a hell of a lot easier just to not make plans. Then you won't get screwed out of them by the department."

"You take vacation around here, that's when they're going to transfer you or screw with you for sure."

> *"I'm saving my vacation time so that if they screw with me, I'll have some time on the books to take care of business."*

Listening to the cynical officers, the victim theme comes through loud and clear. Their whole orientation toward time is from a victim perspective. This doesn't mean these victim officers didn't learn that orientation from reality; in fact, they probably did get screwed out of plans and activities many times over the course of their police careers. However, these officers need to honestly answer this question:

"How often does the agency actually screw you out of your plans?"

Victim officers will respond, "All the time. Every time I make plans, they screw me over." Survivors, on the other hand, might assume a more quantitatively accurate perspective and say, "Oh, 20 or 30 percent of the time they screw up my plans." Survivors will put a number to how many times their personal lives have been invaded by the professional demands of the job. Clearly, the realities are that the personal life of the law enforcement officer will be invaded by the demands of the law enforcement career. Remember my perspective on this issue. "No one escapes their police career with their professional virginity intact. Everyone gets screwed by the agency at least one time."

The difficulty is that victims, early in their careers, can combine the immediate sense of disappointment from having personal plans arbitrarily canceled because of agency needs with the vegetative-like state of the magic chair and cease to aggressively and proactively control their personal lives. Instead of recognizing, as survivors do, that 70 to 80 percent of the time, their plans are *not* canceled, they take a victim orientation toward their personal time and the days become weeks, and weeks become months, with very little other than work being accomplished.

If an officer goes to work, comes home each day, and rides the magic chair for the remainder of his or her personal life, it sets up an interesting mathematical computation:

Let's say the officer does nothing in his or her personal life each day for a thousand days. If you multiply nothing times a thousand, what do you get?

Nothing!

One of the basic reasons the personal lives of many police officers are lost is not due to a conscious effort to cease engaging in off-duty activities, but rather to a loss of a sense of control of the time to do the activities.

The frequency of non-work-related activity diminishes over the first few years of police work until it basically no longer exists. Learning to aggressively control personal time is a fundamental element of becoming an emotional survivor. The officer develops an orientation from which he or she clearly appreciates there is an amount of time each day that the agency controls, but there's also a significant amount of time each day that the officer controls—the time in her or his personal life. The rollercoaster causes the victim officers to abdicate all control of the very manner in which they view their daily personal time. This loss of control clearly facilitates the development of a victim orientation. Beliefs such as "There's never enough time" become the daily orientation of many law enforcement officers. Putting personal time control back in the hands of officers begins with truly understanding the concept of *personal empowerment*.

Time Management and Relationships

Survivors are empowered people. They know what they run each day in their lives and they actually go forth and run it. Victims have a sense of having been wronged and focus in on retribution or retaliation against those they see as the party that victimized them, typically the agency where they are employed. Survivors have a very different orientation toward priorities in life. Although many law enforcement officers would profess that they love their husband, wife, or children, it would be very interesting to see how much time they invest each day in the people they profess to love. Unfortunately, children and domestic partners can become secondary in the life of a law enforcement officer who is oscillating between the two pendulous extremes of the biological rollercoaster.

One law enforcement officer, a fourteen-year veteran, discussed his loss of personal time control and how it affected his marriage:

> *"My wife told me that she knew she was the most*
> *important thing in my life. She just wanted to know if*
> *she was the most important thing in my day."*

The officer went on to relate that his wife's question caused him to take a significant reassessment of his priorities each day. He stated that it was very difficult to spend the entire day highly energized and vigilant, "putting fires out" as a police officer, then return home and give his personal life and the people he loved the attention they deserved and that he wanted to give them. He didn't know how to do it.

The Greatest Accomplishment

An officer who understood the importance of aggressive time management was asked during his retirement dinner by the chief of police, "Looking back on your career, what do you think your greatest accomplishment as a police officer was these last twenty years?"

The officer stated firmly, "I didn't miss one of my three children's basketball games over the years that each of them were in high school."

The chief thought this was a rather unique response and asked him to elaborate. The officer went on, "For me to make each of my three sons' basketball games required more work and proactive scheduling than handling any case or investigation that I had as a police officer. I had to change days off, reschedule off-duty work details, and even beg prosecutors to use me at a different point in their trial. It took a significant effort. As I look back, I have more pride in the fact that I didn't miss even one of my sons' basketball games than any sense of accomplishment in all the idiots I wrote tickets to or arrested."

In many ways this officer is highly justified in his sense of accomplishment and pride in not having missed one of his sons' basketball games. Over the course of his lifetime, his proactive effort and management of his personal time reaped significantly more dividends for his overall emotional survival than a few more hours riding the hypervigilance rollercoaster, either sitting at home watching television or working some off-duty employment detail, ever would have.

The fundamental core issue for survivor law enforcement officers is to possess a belief that they run their personal lives. This is a basic separation in orientation between the victim and the survivor. The victim begins viewing life and personal time as something to be endured until "retirement and I can get away from these assholes and start living my own life." The survivor, on the other hand, has a sense of mastery, empowerment, and control of his or her day-to-day life. People with an aggressive sense of running their own personal lives do not waste time ruminating or obsessing over perceived wrongs by the agency. Rather, they aggressively attempt to live life to the fullest by overcoming the deleterious effects of the biological rollercoaster and the magic chair.

Many young police officers talk about how over the course of the first few years their marriages and relationships change and are redefined. Marriages often end because, from the involved parties' perspective, "We fell out of love with each other." Although on occasion that clearly does happen, how often do marriages end because there is a significant lack of time spent together in joint efforts and activities? That joint activity could be working to achieve some shared goals or just sharing fun with each other during recreational pursuits. Many law enforcement relationships die on the vine because the officer is so caught up in the rollercoaster ride, he or she fails to cultivate the relationship. Relationships that once were dynamic and loving can be destroyed by lack of emotional investment and energy.

Survivors Practice Physical Fitness

The second major element of the survival orientation is an awareness, obtained through training, that the hypervigilance rollercoaster is physiological in nature. Therefore, any remedy will also need to be in part physiological in nature. Physical fitness is not a luxury for law enforcement officers; it's a basic requirement if they are to become emotional survivors. The pendulous swing between the highs and lows of the rollercoaster are the body's way of attempting to recalibrate or balance the effects of the extreme physical reactions caused by hypervigilance. This need to balance, or find homeostasis biologically, is a necessary process and it can be facilitated by aggressive physical fitness.

Physical fitness is not a luxury for law enforcement officers; it's a basic requirement if they are to become emotional survivors.

Although hypervigilance is a necessary worldview if a law enforcement officer is to survive a career that exposes him or her to potential risk each day, the officer does have the option of not passively waiting at the bottom half of the rollercoaster for the effects to correct themselves. Physical fitness will accelerate movement out of the lower reaches of the rollercoaster and back into the normal range of emotion. Physical fitness moves the off-duty officer upward, back between the lines and into the normal range of emotion and social interaction.

Obviously, physical fitness has benefits for a law enforcement officer far beyond breaking the effect of the rollercoaster. Physical fitness, in terms of muscular flexibility and the possession of the necessary dynamic strength to perform the job duties, is fundamental for the officer's physical survival. Therefore, an officer who is a physical and an emotional survivor lives his or her personal life not in the depressive-like ranges at the bottom of the rollercoaster but rather between the lines. They're spontaneous, outgoing, and engaged in activities.

What Kind of Exercise?

For officers to move up from the bottom of the rollercoaster back within the normal range necessitates a physical intervention. The physical intervention can be accomplished by moderate aerobic exercise. Approximately thirty to forty minutes of aerobic activity, four to five times per week, appears to be adequate in increasing an officer's off-duty activity levels. Thirty to forty minutes of aerobic activity raises the bottom portion of the rollercoaster back within the normal limits. The impact of exercise on the biological rollercoaster is shown in the figure below:

The Effect of Exercise on the
Biological Rollercoaster

On Duty

Alive, Alert, Energetic, Involved, Humorous

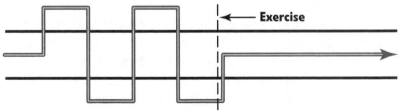

Tired, Detached, Isolated, Apathetic

Off Duty

Notice the arrow has moved from the bottom of the rollercoaster back to the normal range. The impact of exercise on the hypervigilance rollercoaster is one of the paradoxes of the physiological effects of hypervigilance. If you were physically exhausted from the expenditure of muscular energy and then returned to your personal life and physically exercised, this exercise would only further enhance your sense of exhaustion. The sense of detachment, isolation, fatigue, and apathy that typify the bottom reaches of the hypervigilance rollercoaster, however, respond positively to physical exercise. Ask any group of law enforcement officers how they feel after they exercise and they inevitably respond: "Tired, but a lot better." Physical exercise not only raises the behavioral activity level of the officer, it also has significant stress-reducing components that give the officer a sense of relaxation and generalized well-being.

Moderate physical exercise is also an essential element in any program of anger reduction. The physiological consequence of hypervigilance leaves law enforcement officers feeling detached, isolated, and apathetic to social interaction; however, it can also leave them with a sense of irritability, frustration, and emotional volatility. One of the tragedies facing law enforcement families is officers returning home after dealing with unsolvable social problems only to have the frustration, irritability, and anger caused by the job transferred into domestic violence after experiencing a normal disagreement or annoyance at home. Officers who are angry often transfer that emotional distress into physically inappropriate behavior. Officers and families say things they can't take back and, unfortunately, this can lead to acts of physical violence. Not only is moderate physical fitness a key element in breaking the destructive aspects of the biological rollercoaster, it also provides officers a much needed physical outlet and relief valve to drain the effects of generalized job stress, and it helps maintain an overall wellness-based lifestyle.

The insight the officer and family obtain through training in emotional survival shows them how terribly important a continuing physical fitness and exercise program can be. Many police officers will discuss physical fitness after ten years as officers and say, "I usta be very fit. I ran every day. I usta go to the gym." The "I usta" syndrome plays a major role in the disappearance and reduction of physical fitness in the lives of law enforcement officers.

Many law enforcement agencies in recent years have begun stressing physical fitness and providing workout areas or exercise rooms for personnel. Unfortunately, no small number of these agencies have invested their monetary resources into weight-lifting and other strength-related equipment, which, although highly beneficial for the health and strength of the officer, do not have as direct an effect on the hypervigilance rollercoaster as does aerobic exercise.

Aerobic exercise is any exercise that is rhythmic and repetitive and places the emphasis on the exchange of oxygen and carbon dioxide. It focuses on the cardiovascular system and places the target heart rate as a goal of exercise. Aerobic exercises such as walking, biking, basketball, racquetball, or exercise involving specialized aerobic equipment are readily available for officers.

Resistance to Exercise

Law enforcement officers typically begin their careers highly knowledgeable and sophisticated in terms of physical fitness. As the years pass and the biological rollercoaster takes its toll, however, officers stop applying their knowledge of physical fitness and begin living a sedentary off-duty lifestyle, which typifies too many law enforcement officers' day-to-day existence. Most officers do not need to be convinced of the benefits of exercise. They know the effects of exercise from previous stages in their lives. They *do* need help in making the exercise happen. They need to be made aware through emotional survival training of the necessity of physical fitness across their career and life spans as a means of providing significant emotional assistance. Any intervention by an agency that helps its personnel develop programs of physical fitness plays a major role in the overall survival of its officers.

Many law enforcement officers are resistant to physical fitness. Some officers are aggressively resistant to the idea of physical fitness and even internalize it into their worldview. It's not uncommon to hear officers say:

"If they want me to jog, how come they give me a patrol car?"

"If they're going to make me exercise, they're going to pay me while I'm doing it."

It's interesting how many officers, even when their agency allots a set number of hours per month for physical fitness, still resist the concept of aggressively taking a sense of responsibility for and control of their day-to-day physical activity. One of the significant benefits of a maintained and disciplined physical fitness program is that it sets a period of time each day during which the officer puts the demands of police work on the back burner and takes responsibility for his or her own behavior—the very act of exercising. A sustained physical fitness program will not be found in the day-to-day life of an individual who views the world as a victim and who doesn't have proactive and disciplined time management. The victim officer will say, "I know I need to exercise, but I just can't find the time." The individual who sets aside time four or five times each week to take responsibility for his or her physical fitness will also take responsibility for other personal life aspects that previously had been put on the back burner or abandoned. The very act of engaging in physical fitness means the officer is taking control and responsibility for his or her time and actions each day.

> The very act of engaging in physical fitness means the officer is taking control and responsibility for his or her time and actions each day.

Survivors Control Their Financial Well-Being

One surprising aspect of physical fitness appears to be that officers who aggressively practice physical fitness and pursue physical activities in their personal lives appear to be somewhat more stable financially. The answer to this might lie in some simple behavioral observations. When marketing professionals observe financial transactions, they note some significant gender differences in spending behavior. Marketing research relates that, in general, if two or three women are socializing and they are mildly depressed or not having a good day, they frequently decide to go shopping. The behavioral and marketing researchers on Madison Avenue have known this observation to be true for many years. They have clearly established that certain individuals, when feeling mildly depressed or unfocused, can find themselves feeling more energetic if they purchase something. This form of "retail therapy" does have distinct gender differences. Women tend to make small ticket purchases, things that can be absorbed within the next budget cycle. Small items achieve the desired emotional response of "feeling better, feeling more alive." This traditionally female gender approach to making purchases is more conservative and rarely involves a major purchase. Small purchases get the job done in terms of mood elevation. The traditionally male counterpart to this behavior, however, does not appear to be as simple nor as conservative. Males do not appear to like to "go shopping" but they do enjoy "buying stuff." What kinds of stuff do they enjoy buying? The male's stuff appears to be big-ticket items—boats, cars, pickup trucks, motor homes, campers, and maybe some power tools. The typical law enforcement spending pattern, unfortunately, appears to be more closely linked to the traditional male spending pattern. The items officers tend to purchase are large, and they are typically not absorbed within the next budget cycle. It does feel good to make the purchase, however:

> *"Why don't you come over and check out my new pickup truck? Man, I tell you what, this truck is just great. It has the new diesel engine and 4 x 4 transmission. I just love driving this truck. It's got the all-leather-interior package. It's a great truck. Man, I just love driving around in it."*

How long does this "great" feeling last?
Until the first payment!
How long do the payments last?
Four or five years.

How are those payments going to be made considering this purchase is not easily absorbed within the routine family budget cycle? The answer, again, is quite clear:

> *Work a few extra off-duty jobs or grab as much overtime as possible to make the payments.*

This spending pattern can represent a vicious cycle that affects many officers and families who have not been trained in emotional survival. These families often fall prey to *stress-related consumerism*.

The Stress–Related Consumerism Cycle
Stress-related consumerism is an officer's attempt to move from the bottom reaches of the biological rollercoaster to the top by making

novelty purchases. The cycle can become quite overwhelming for some officers who purchase a new vehicle or recreational toy and find themselves working every available off-duty job or taking all the available overtime in order to meet the financial obligations of the purchase. The cycle can become quite consuming. The officer's financial life can become one continuous interaction between making a major purchase that is designed to alleviate some psychological distress and provide some recreational panacea and the need to be forever increasing the number of off-duty jobs and overtime hours to address the new financial obligation. A vicious financial and off-duty work-related cycle has begun.

This cycle robs the officer of any sense of financial security across the span of the occupational career. Many officers, without having a sense of proactive control of their finances, experience significant distress economically, in spite of enjoying an occupational career that is generally free of lay-offs and downsizing, with excellent retirement and medical benefits. Many officers have a lack of financial sophistication in reviewing their economic status. Living the rollercoaster across a career can produce a middle-aged law enforcement officer whose level of knowledge and awareness economically is not significantly greater than what typified the beginning of the career ten or fifteen years earlier. Quite frequently the financial security of the law enforcement retirement program is a major factor in why a significant number of individuals remain in the law enforcement field long after the attractiveness or novelty of the job has passed. Ironically, the desire to obtain financial security in many officers is often limited to valuing only the retirement itself. Many law enforcement agencies provide excellent financial benefit packages, including deferred compensation programs, but often do not take adequate time to inform and educate their employees of the potential financial benefits available.

Financial frustration at an individual level can be transferred into collective bargaining unit frustrations with the management of an organization. Financial difficulties, as seen by an officer lacking in a sophisticated awareness of his or her financial status, on more than one occasion have led to inappropriate ethical and even criminal violations of trust relationships when an officer takes inappropriate actions, motivated by short-term financial gain. Providing law enforcement officers with a sophisticated awareness of the potential financial benefit packages available, as is done in the private sector, would create an increased sense of financial security as officers approach the latter years of their law enforcement careers. A sense of appreciation of financial security would also reduce anger and frustration, as well as the need to continuously work second jobs to support short-term, emotionally generated purchases. Officers who have a sense of financial security are in a position to free themselves of anger and frustration at their employers and continue to invest energy into the professional goals that typified the earlier years of their careers.

Survivors Have Multiple Roles in Their Lives

One of the most difficult aspects of being a law enforcement officer is the need to strike a balance between being a highly effective law enforcement professional and at the same time an available friend, spouse, or parent outside of the law enforcement role. This capacity to balance multiple significant emotional roles in one's life is the central defining aspect of an emotional survivor versus an emotional victim. The emotional victim, as previous chapters illuminate, is singularly defined by the police role. All emotional and psychological needs are closely linked to the law enforcement role. As demonstrated by case histories in previous chapters, the officer does not control the law enforcement role. If lack of control is one of the central components of the victim, then by definition the law enforcement officer whose life view is singularly defined by being a law enforcement officer is the most prone to being a victim. Many officers who have approached their entire law enforcement career enthusiastic, positively motivated, and highly energized about the job can unknowingly be victim-prone officers. Many times this victim-prone officer is operating from a perspective of emotional naiveté and unawareness of what could be lurking around the corner with any change in the organization. One example of a victim-prone officer is Commander Vasquez, in the following case study.

Case History

Commander Vasquez is an eighteen-year patrol-division commander of a medium-size police department. Throughout the course of his career, he has enthusiastically met every professional challenge that the organization has put before him. Commander Vasquez's average work week far exceeds the typical forty hours. Quite often several nights per week he is available to the men and women of his command. He understands the basic tenets of leadership and practices them quite well. Commander Vasquez easily is the most respected member of the command staff at his organization. The men and women who work for Commander Vasquez know that he cares about them, that he is an individual of honesty and integrity. The line personnel of the agency often say: "If you were disciplined by Commander Vasquez, you deserved it. He doesn't play games with the people who work for him."

Commander Vasquez's career at one level is highly successful. He enjoys the respect of rank-and-file law enforcement officers as well as colleagues within the command staff. Commander Vasquez pursued an advanced education, over the course of his career, obtaining a master's degree in public administration. He is also fortunate enough to be able to attend the FBI National Academy in Quantico, Virginia, and has a significant network of law enforcement colleagues at a national level.

From all outside views, Commander Vasquez would be considered a successful law enforcement officer. However, during Commander Vasquez's eighteenth year of employment, the chief of police for whom he works retires and is replaced by an individual who was an assistant chief at a major city police department from another part of the country. Commander Vasquez has just begun his attendance at the FBI National Academy when the new chief arrives at his agency to assume the position of chief of police. Commander Vasquez's absence over the course of the new chief of police's first three months of tenure creates a situation in which the new chief of police has created friendships with several other members of the command staff and considers Commander Vasquez somewhat of an unknown entity and often refers to him at command meetings as "the commander we have back at the NA."

Upon returning from his three-month stint at the National Academy, Commander Vasquez finds he's been transferred to a new command position in another area of the agency. This particular transfer does not trouble Commander Vasquez, who views his position with the agency with flexibility, and he meets his new position with enthusiasm.

Commander Vasquez realizes that he has been successful throughout his career by approaching his tasks with enthusiasm, motivation, and dedication to his position as a law enforcement commander. Although successful in his new command position, Commander Vasquez begins noticing that the new chief of police operates from an ethical frame of reference that is somewhat different from what had typified the agency under the old chief of police. Commander Vasquez believes in operating above reproach and feels strongly that interaction with the public, subordinate officers, or command colleagues should always be predicated on honesty and integrity. It becomes quite apparent to Commander Vasquez that the new chief of police values political loyalty and a network of sycophants more than professional integrity. Commander Vasquez, during executive retreats on more than one occasion, points out respectfully that programs the new chief of police is considering are somewhat self-serving for the police department and lack the sense of community need and integrity that Commander Vasquez believes are core to the manner in which the agency serves the public. The present chief of police advises Commander Vasquez that it is not his concern whether the program is based on integrity or not and that Commander Vasquez should do what he is told if he wants to retain his command or the chief of police would find somebody else who would do it. Commander Vasquez at no point engages in disrespectful interaction with the chief of police, but he soon finds himself being removed from areas of professional responsibility that he values. A confidante advises Commander Vasquez that the new chief of police considers him untrustworthy.

While functioning as a force commander (a rotating temporary assignment that all command personnel do one shift per month), Commander Vasquez supervises the dispatching of patrol officers to the city manager's residence for a domestic violence incident. Upon arriving at the location of the call, Commander Vasquez is met by a patrol sergeant and three patrol officers who inform him that the city manager has physically assaulted his wife to the extent that she would require minor medical attention. Commander Vasquez

(continued)

reminds the patrol sergeant of the departmental policy and state statutes concerning domestic violence incidents and the need for a mandatory physical arrest of the city manager. The officers under Commander Vasquez's direction take the city manager into custody. Commander Vasquez believes the arrest is absolutely appropriate, is based on probable cause and the evidence at the scene, and does not reflect either an absence of law enforcement action taken nor preferential treatment toward the city manager. Upon hearing of the physical arrest of the city manager, however, the chief of police informally admonishes Commander Vasquez, informing him that the organization has "an institutional memory."

During the next months, Commander Vasquez finds his evaluations reflect ratings of below satisfactory performance, a rating that Commander Vasquez has never received in his prior eighteen years of law enforcement service. Commander Vasquez believes that if he continues to use the traits of dedication, motivation, and integrity that have typified his career, he will soon convince the new chief of police that his performance as a law enforcement officer is based on integrity and not politics. Quite obviously, Commander Vasquez operates ethically and professionally from a different frame of reference than does the new chief of police. Commander Vasquez continues to find himself embroiled in informal discipline and being professionally ostracized by the new chief. As the months continue and as he becomes convinced that the chief of police is an ethically bankrupt individual, Commander Vasquez's attitude toward the chief becomes confrontational. He begins assuming a rather defensive posture and eventually must retain an attorney to protect his professional position when the chief of police begins demotional proceedings against him for reasons lacking any objective foundation.

As the confrontation with the new chief of police develops and intensifies, it becomes quite apparent that Commander Vasquez lacks the emotional support systems that would typify an emotional survivor. His career has been highly successful and he does not have any significant bumps in the road over the past two decades of being a law enforcement officer. He sees the department only in a positive light and believes he has always been treated fairly by the agency. But for the first time in Commander Vasquez's life, he finds himself becoming disenchanted and angry, and he feels ostracized by the inner circle of individuals who now run the police department. Commander Vasquez begins realizing that for the past eighteen years of his life, the police department has been his central focus. He has not developed significant support systems outside of law enforcement. Commander Vasquez does not have any friends outside of law enforcement personnel. He does not belong to any established spiritual worship community. He does not have any driving recreational pursuits or a significant program of physical fitness.

As the confrontations with the chief of police and his band of sycophants begin increasing, Commander Vasquez finds himself ruminating and becoming obsessed with the manner in which the new chief of police is treating him. He becomes quite agitated in his personal life. He begins experiencing a sleep disorder because he spends his nights contemplating what is taking place in his professional life, and he becomes increasingly enraged. In basic terms, Commander Vasquez has lived his entire life for the past two decades by putting all of his emotional needs in the basket called *police work*, and now, for the first time in his career, he realizes he does not hold the handle to that basket—his career. All the skills that worked previously for Commander Vasquez—honesty, integrity, hard work, dedication, and motivation—do not enable him to overcome the burden of having to work for a basically politically dishonest chief of police. Retirement for Commander Vasquez is at a minimum three years in the future and he does not appear to have any outlets other than police work in which to invest his energy. Commander Vasquez's life has turned from being basically a positive, enthusiastic one to a life consumed by anger, frustration, hostility, and resentment toward the manner in which he is being treated by an agency that he was quite willing to say, a few years ago, that he loved.

Commander Vasquez's dilemma is not uncommon in law enforcement at all. Honest and dedicated law enforcement officers have a difficult time accepting political favoritism, cronyism, disloyalty, and dishonesty. Unfortunately, many good men and women can find themselves confronted with the paradox of being emotionally overinvested and defining themselves as law enforcement officers, yet at the same time beginning to hate the role. If you hate the role of police officer and at the same time you define yourself only by the role of police officer, you begin a cycle of self-hatred and destructiveness. Commander Vasquez clearly has significant deficits in non-police-related roles in his life. The emotional rollercoaster, as well as a basic love of police work, have combined to produce a deficiency of outside support systems in his life. Although Commander Vasquez is married, he and his wife have not established any ongoing social or recreational pursuits they share in common. She has her own profession, as does Commander Vasquez. They live rather independent lives. His two children are both away at college and, for the first time in his life, Commander Vasquez finds himself becoming angry, frustrated, and depressed about his present position. He looks forward to retirement, not so much from a position of enthusiasm for post-retirement life, but mainly as a way to "get away from the chief."

> *If you hate the role of police officer and at the same time you define yourself only by the role of police officer, you begin a cycle of self-hatred and destructiveness.*

Survivors have other roles in their lives. Although at the surface level Commander Vasquez was successful, positive, and enthusiastic for the majority of his career, he is basically a victim waiting to happen. Commander Vasquez does not have a significant amount of his life that is truly in his hands. Quite obviously he controls his dedication, his professionalism, and how well he does his job, but he does not have a well-developed social network outside of police work. He also does not have any recreational pursuits or physical fitness strategies to help him deal with the social and physical confrontations he is facing.

Quite often, law enforcement officers, when reviewing their career, will speak about a change from "loving the job" to "hating this place." Both attitudes, in all likelihood, would typify overinvestment emotionally. Having a positive, enthusiastic dedication toward police work while at the same time having a positive, enthusiastic dedication toward other aspects of one's life would typify balance, the central trait of the survivor. Keeping all emotional eggs in one basket, whether those are eggs marked "love" or marked "hate," is the central trait of the victim. Learning the skills to balance investment in the police role with investment in personal life roles is what defines a survivor. Having other roles in life that the officer truly controls reduces the feeling of vulnerability, helplessness, and being emotionally at risk to the agency that typifies many victim officers. The survivor has a balanced emotional investment. This investment continues over many years of productive police work. It's not so much that the survivor officer has learned to turn off police work at the end of the shift as it is that he or she has learned to turn on the other roles. The other roles are not merely pastimes or idle activities for the survivor law enforcement officers; they are truly emotionally invested dimensions in officers' lives. These other roles are dimensions of life in which the officers have a sense of passion and concern and, most important, control and self-determination.

Decide to Survive

Being the best law enforcement officer one can be is very important to the survivor officer, but so is being

- the best mother
- the best father
- the best husband
- the best wife
- the best community member
- the best golfer
- the best fly fisherman
- the best little league coach
- the best scout leader

The officers who make police work their lives are only coasting through a career and really don't have a strategy to be emotional survivors. They are only hoping that they don't get screwed by

- the agency
- the chief
- the sheriff
- the special agent in charge

They forget the one basic rule about the police career:

Nobody, but nobody, escapes with their professional virginity intact. Everyone gets screwed at least one time.

Survivors place the central issues in their lives in their own control. They understand what they control and what the agency controls. Once officers reach the point of being emotional survivors, they experience a significant reduction in anxiety and defensiveness. They focus on being the best officers they can be and then move on to more important things. Survivors make decisions from their core values, not from situational values, so they are typically free of facing significant disciplinary attention. On occasion, even though they are deserving of

> *Survivors place the central issues in their lives in their own control. They understand what they control and what the agency controls.*

it, they are not promoted or they are not chosen for the assignment they would like to have received, but they are still the most successful officers.

Emotional survivors may appear to finish in last place, but that is because they are usually running a different race.

Becoming an emotional survivor can be a decision an officer makes at any point in a law enforcement career. On occasion, even a retired law enforcement professional must learn the strategies and attributes of becoming an emotional survivor to undo emotional damage that developed years, even decades, before. Police families can practice the skills of being survivor families, putting the priorities and events of the lives of family members well above the events taking place at the law enforcement agency. The journey through a law enforcement career does not have to lead to the devastation and loss that it so often does. Just as law enforcement professionals practice street survival, they must practice emotional survival—they only need to be shown and mentored and modeled across the years of service.

The Officer's Legacy

In looking at how many officers live life as either victims or survivors, I'd like to point out two cases of two good officers making very different choices.

Case History

A chief of a medium-size police agency calls to ask me to help the family of a terminally ill officer. The chief relates that his officer has but a few weeks remaining to live and is requesting that his twenty-five-year-old son come to the hospice so the officer can make his peace with his son and say goodbye. The chief relates to me that the son has not spoken to his father since the son turned eighteen and left home after some turbulent teenage years. The chief had spoken to the son and attempted on his own to convince him to visit his father, but on each occasion the son refused. The chief asks if I would attempt to convince the son to see his dying father.

I travel for a day to meet with the son. I arrive unannounced at the son's home and ask to speak with him. Upon introducing myself and telling the son that I am there to talk to him about his father, the son states, "You're here to tell me my father's dead, aren't you?"

I reply, "No, but you really ought to go see him."

To this rather inappropriate statement, the son becomes enraged and begins yelling at me to leave, saying I have no right to impose my opinion on matters that do not pertain to me. The son becomes physically threatening and tells me, "Get off my place before I kick your ass!"

After I tell him I've traveled a few hundred miles to talk to him about this, the son backs off and says, "Well, hell, you came that far, I'll listen to what you have to say." The son, however, does the talking:

"You want to know about my father, well, I'll tell you about my father. The only thing I remember about him growing up was I was constantly told if I didn't straighten up, I was going to grow up to be a 'total asshole.' I have no memory of him helping me with school, coming to any of my football or basketball games, or anything. Hell, he was always too busy with his damn police work. When I got old enough to not have to take his bullshit anymore, things got real tense around the house. I left home the day after graduation from high school, and I haven't spoken a word to him since then, and I have no intention of talking to him now. I'm sorry he's real sick, but it just isn't my problem. I closed the book on him seven years ago and I'm not going to open it again."

I talk to him for close to three hours and the young man doesn't budge an inch. I tell him, "It would take you about fifteen minutes out of your way to stop at the hospice and see your father. If it is a total waste of time, as you think it will be for you, then all you've wasted is fifteen minutes; but when your father is gone, you'll never get that chance again." To this the son replies, "I'm not going to give it fifteen seconds. The book is closed. You tell my mother that when he is gone, I'll help her any way I can."

In spite of my attempts and discussion, the son refuses to see his father and I leave unsuccessful. After seeing the son, I talk with the

(continued)

chief who had requested my involvement and ask him to tell me about his officer.

The chief replies, "I don't know what the hell is wrong with that son of his. My officer is one of the best men I have ever known in my lifetime. He is a caring and compassionate person. He is active in our school programs working with kids. He is involved in our officers' association and helps put on a toy drive every Christmas for the poor kids in our town, and every Thanksgiving, he and a handful of other officers help sponsor a food drive and pass out boxes of food and turkeys to families that can't afford a holiday meal. I just don't know what the hell is wrong with that boy of his."

I say I am sorry I couldn't convince the son to visit his father and leave to begin the trip back home. While traveling home, I reflect on why the son wouldn't visit the hospice and see his father. In spite of the conflicts that previously existed, the son's visit would make the officer's last days more comfortable by possibly enabling the officer to have closure and maybe discuss and try to make amends for the difficulties that typified their father-son relationship. I later learn from the chief that the father-son meeting never took place. It seems like such a waste. How do two people become so estranged? I wonder if the officer, whom the chief of police described as a compassionate man who cared about people, was the same man the son knew. Was the chief describing the man at the top of the rollercoaster and the son describing the man at the bottom of the rollercoaster? Did they even know the same person?

Case History

Not long after the case history above takes place, a police agency requests that I assist in a death notification of an officer who died in a motor vehicle accident while in another city. I go to the home along with the chief of police and a chaplain. The young woman being told her husband will never come home again is approximately thirty-five years old with two adolescent children.

I visit with the family several times during the next few months. Obviously, she is devastated and overwhelmed by the emotional trauma of the situation, but her support systems of family, friends, and fellow church members appear to be immensely helping her deal with her grief and loss.

On one visit to the home, I need to borrow the family telephone to return a call. In the kitchen, I notice a small placard taped under the wall-mounted telephone that reads:

"This is a Career not a Crusade."

I ask the widow about the placard's meaning and she responds, "Oh, I should take that down, but I just don't have the courage. My husband put it up there, half as a joke and half as a reminder. It started down at the agency where he had pictures of his family on his desk and some of the other detectives had pictures of loads of narcotics they had seized—you know the cops call them the 'glory shots.' He had the family pictures on his desk and they teased him about it. The other guys at the agency put up a little sign that said, 'So much Cocaine, such little Time,' and that was when my husband put up the sign at the office: 'This is a Career not a Crusade.' It all started as a joke, but I think it was pretty serious to him.

"He loved working as a cop, but he saw so many of his friends lose marriages and families. They all would go out for a beer after work. My husband would go most of the time, but he was usually the first to leave and come home. He really loved being a cop, but you know he always remembered the family. I might forget a birthday, anniversary, or something. He never did. If he had to work on Thanksgiving, then we had our meal the day before or the day after, but we had our Thanksgiving as a family. Our Christmas might be December 23rd because of his job, but we had our family Christmas. I think he made just about every parent-teacher meeting or school event; some he couldn't make, but he sure tried. I miss him terribly, but I had such a wonderful life with him."

As I listen to this young widow recounting her husband's life as an officer and as a father and husband, I am struck by just one word of her story:

*"I **had** such a wonderful life with him."*

On other occasions, I have spoken to spouses or parents who have lost law enforcement loved ones, and the words are often different than those spoken by the widow in the above case history. So often the words are "I miss him terribly, and he could have retired last year, and then we were going to have our time," or "In five years we were going to retire and move upstate and then it would be our time." This young woman in the above case history told a story of an excellent law enforcement officer who must have seen life as a survivor. They *had* such a wonderful life together. They lived in the present. They took advantage of every moment of their family and personal time, and at the same time he was a highly productive officer. He apparently had the strategies to break the rollercoaster. His life was full, and he left a family that missed and valued him.

The question could be asked:

"Which officer loved his family and children more, the officer in the first case whose son wouldn't visit him as he died, or the second officer, who saw police work as a 'career not a crusade'?"

In my opinion, they *both* loved their families and children. They were probably both good, decent men and hardworking law enforcement officers. Unfortunately, one didn't have an orientation through training in emotional survival and his victim outlook came into the home and destroyed his relationship with his son. The other officer left a wife and two children who knew he loved them, not just with his emotions, but also with his behavior and time. The second officer's child is presently a law enforcement officer at the father's agency. The second officer knew how to break the rollercoaster and live life. Although tragically he died too young, he lived life as a survivor.

About the Author

Dr. Kevin M. Gilmartin is a behavioral scientist specializing in law enforcement–related issues. He is a principal and co-founder of Gilmartin, Harris, and Associates, a behavioral sciences/management consulting company specializing in law enforcement/public safety consultation. He previously spent twenty years working in law enforcement in Tucson, Arizona. During his tenure he supervised the Hostage Negotiations Team and the Behavioral Sciences Unit. He is a former recipient of the International Association of Chiefs of Police (IACP)– *Parade Magazine* National Police Officer Citation Award for contributions during hostage negotiations.

He presently maintains a consulting relationship with public safety and law enforcement agencies nationally in the United States and in Canada. He is an instructor at the FBI Academy's Law Enforcement Executive Development Institute (LEEDS or EDI). He is an adjunct instructor at Cornell University's New York State School of Industrial and Labor Relations, the University of Massachusetts Police Leadership Institute, Federal Law Enforcement Training Center in Glynco, Georgia, and Sam Houston State University's Law Enforcement Management Institute of Texas. He is retained as a consultant to several federal-agency national-critical-incident response teams. He is a charter member of the IACP Psychological Services Section and former vice president of the Society of Police and Criminal Psychology. The Department of Justice, the FBI, and International Association of Chiefs of Police have published his work. He holds a doctoral degree in Clinical Psychology from the University of Arizona. He is a veteran of the U.S. Marine Corps and resides in Tucson, Arizona, and Salem, Oregon.

E-S Press

Order Form

Additional copies of *Emotional Survival for Law Enforcement* are available from E-S Press. Mail in this order form with payment or contact us by fax, e-mail, or through our website to receive one or more copies. (Quantity discounts are available upon request.)

Shipping and Handling:
Please add to the total price $5.00 for the first book and $1.00 for each additional book. Add $6.00 for the first book and $1.50 for each additional book for priority delivery or delivery to Canada. Send payment with the order form below to

E-S Press
8340 N. Thornydale Rd. #110-314
Tucson, Arizona 85741-1162

We also accept orders by fax or e-mail (please be sure to include the information requested in the orderblank below):

Tel.: 520-744-0703
Cell: 520-977-6729
Fax: 520-744-9298
E-mail: espresstucson@aol.com

Or visit our website: **www.EmotionalSurvival.com**

- -

Name: _____

Address: _____

City: _____

State: _____

ZIP: _____

Telephone: _____

I would like _____ books @ $19.95 each.

Payment:
(Please do not send cash.)
☐ Check or money order payable to E-S Press is enclosed
☐ Please charge my ☐ Visa or ☐ Mastercard

Account #:_____   Exp. Date: _____

Signature: _____